Group Work with the Aged

Group Work with the Aged

by

SUSAN H. KUBIE

and

GERTRUDE LANDAU

International Universities Press, Inc.

New York   New York

To the Members of Hodson Center

CONTENTS

Preface

When the authors set themselves the task of surveying what only nine years ago was a wholly new experiment in social welfare, it was with the liveliest awareness that their experience and their interest would be focused on what was already a second stage of this innovation. What went before was a stage harder to record since it was a period of germination in which a new area of human need was recognized.

It is the special achievement of one man, Harry A. Levine, which placed these authors in a position to report not only a change in the general status of the aged in our community today, but the heartening developments and rehabilitation of so many individuals who have been involved in center programs. It was his imagination about ways of meeting their needs which crystallized into the first plans for a Day Center —and his tireless efforts in organizing a community response to their problems which created not only the center which we describe but a growing chain of such centers as their value proved itself.

His credo "creative energy is ageless" has been a challenge wherever the static concept of old age imprisoned its hapless victims in indifference and neglect. He has not only awakened communities to their plight but has also been able to create for their benefit a new cooperation between public and private social agencies wherever such agencies could fruitfully combine their services to benefit this new group of clients.

It is through leadership such as that of Harry A. Levine that the ever-growing numbers of the aged may look to a better future in which social planning for the later years will be both wider in scope and more intensive.

CHAPTER ONE

Introduction

Several reasons have impelled the authors to describe the experience of working for nine years in a recreation center for the aged. The first was personal, since a survey of these accumulated years promised to objectify an experience which had been daily, continuous, and unendingly varied. We hoped by giving ourselves an accounting of the many and exciting changes which transformed that early gathering of bewildered and diffident old people into today's confident and cohesive community, to sharpen our understanding of the role we played in those changes. In this respect the labor of examining our records has been richly rewarding.

Another reason for undertaking such a task was our realization that our experience was in some ways unique and shaped by circumstances which would not be duplicated again. For, nine years ago, a recreation center for the aged was an innovation. It was a new idea to those who started this center, to each of the staff who was to serve it and to the clients who were to make use of it. This made each stage of the experience a daily exploration in methods, in setting of goals, in understanding our clients. Neither clients nor staff knew what to expect, of themselves, of each other or of the project. Their continuous, daily contact was a shared experience in which the first handful of members was increasingly drawn together, while the staff, as both observers and participants in that process, experimented in facilitating it. By so doing the staff deepened its understanding of these older people.

Above all the staff members came to see that old people

react in the same way to gratifications and frustrations, to needs and to opportunities for social development as do all human beings whatever their age.

This latter observation, that old people react on the same principles as all people may hardly seem a major discovery. Yet it is significant of the specific factors which effect their status in our culture that this obvious fact has not been clearly anticipated. Moreover, it seems to be the fate of most explorations into new fields of social welfare that the unique features of the new problems are more apparent than the universal similarities and that basic principles, formulated in one field, are only slowly rediscovered behind the unfamiliar features of a new one.

The staff made this discovery slowly and piece-meal for at the time the center was started the problem of the aged was just beginning to force itself on public attention. The center was a first step in recognizing this problem and as it has grown as a social institution, its development has been paralleled by the community's awareness and growing body of knowledge about old age. The Department of Welfare workers who started the project saw one set of problems and one kind of older person—those who received public assistance. They saw them in the particular circumstances of a large city where arbitrary retirement from work, crowded living conditions and their longevity made their loneliness a conspicuous condition. Therefore these workers concentrated on bringing them together by providing a meeting place.

These circumstances are duplicated in cities throughout the country, and so, today are recreation centers. But these new centers today are set up with a much clearer orientation about their purpose, a body of experience about the methods to use and a knowledge of the results to be expected.

Since this knowledge about the aged is both general and recent, we also felt that it would be timely to report the development of this first project. We hoped that the records of our observations would yield significant facts, types of reactions and patterns of changes in behavior which would lead to generalizations of value to our co-workers in this field, as well as to the growing numbers of people who are becoming interested in old age.

We had to work as practitioners without the benefit of the many disciplines and techniques which already had been brought to bear on other areas of human behavior. The time cannot be far off when such gatherings of older citizens will be used for special studies that will greatly enrich our professional equipment. Psychology, psychiatry and medicine could tell us much more about these people which now we do not know. Sociological studies of these groups and the backgrounds from which they come would supply both methods and principles of observation which would guide our practices and make our observations more fruitful. For, as it has been said, "What we see grows with what we are trained to see and in turn helps the latter to grow."

But meanwhile, since leisure time programs for the aged are springing up throughout the country, we felt that a report of our experience, the record of our tentative experiments, their sometimes successes, their sometimes failures, would be useful in shortening the trial and error periods which inevitably would occur in such projects.

We do not believe that a vastly greater coordination of knowledge will ever supply us with a simple set of rules of practice. Professional skill in working with human beings will always be an art—that is a blend of knowledge, training and intuition. Therefore we not only wanted to give as full and frank an account as possible of what knowledge we accumulated and what professional methods we applied but also the role which our perceptions and our feelings about our clients played in the growth of this center from its beginnings into the large community it is today.

Finally and not least, our survey pointed up for the authors the wider implications of the experience in which we had been immersed. We came to realize that our clients, being the least privileged and therefore the most conspicuous victims of society's prolonged rejection of the aged, had made a social contribution of heartening significance. If these people, so damaged by loneliness and neglect, could still change and grow, then the new longevity which is an outstanding phenomenon of our time, holds a promise for our society beyond anything we have yet taken into account.

CHAPTER TWO

Beginnings

We shall not dwell on the preliminary planning nor the opening of the center. Credit for leadership in creating this social innovation belongs, as we have said, to the Department of Welfare. It is no easy task to recognize a new field for social betterment, to conceive an appropriate plan, to enlist the needed joint cooperation of both a city department and community sponsorship—and then to bring that plan into actuality. All this was done by those farsighted workers, and if we seem to present baldly what was an achievement of imagination, practicality and social pioneering, it is only because these reporters were drawn into the picture at a later date, and further because one of the originators of the project had already and ably described those beginnings. We therefore start with our own records, including only one point from the time of the opening—namely the number of old people who came by invitation from their workers. There were some 350 present on that day. This is a fact to note, since six months later, when it was decided that permanent professional leadership was necessary, the reason was primarily because this initial attendance had dwindled to a fraction of that figure.

The organizers of the project, besides securing a meeting place, had contributed games, had suggested the serving of refreshments to foster sociability, and having gathered the old people together, expected that they could manage by themselves. They had in this way provided them with a more sociable means of passing time, which then seemed adequate provision. No one had thought beyond this point. Yet one of the characteristics of these older people—which was to be a major focus of the first workers' efforts—was now responsible for the diminishing attendance, namely, the tendency of one or two to be self-assertive at the expense of others. The one in whom this drive was the strongest took over the management of the club. Those who submitted passively remained; those who felt this as a renewed frustration left, and this fact was responsible for providing the first professional supervision.

The social worker who was assigned to this group had no precedents to guide her procedure—to tell her what to anticipate, or to suggest what should be the goals of this innovation. She had been told that one of the members, Miss Hardy, had taken a leading role at the club, and that a Mr. Lowden was likewise a key figure among the men; that all but a few of those attending had been referred from the Department of Welfare and were receiving Old Age Assistance. Other than that she did not know what to expect, whether she would find them very old and infirm, or capable and energetic; from what social, economic or national backgrounds they came; how they would look or act—in short, *nothing*.

Since the founding of the club the locale had been changed and the members were now gathered together in a large ground floor room of an old public building. The walls had not been painted in twenty years, the furnishings were a collection of cast-offs, the cooking arrangements an old two-burner electric stove.

During the first fortnight the worker learned the following data in regard to the members:

Of the 40 members, 27 were men and 13 were women. The average age was 71.8 years; the range from 60 to 86 years. There were 3 couples, 9 married men, 14 widowers, 6 widows, 1 single man and 4 single women.

Of these 40 people, 35 were receiving Old Age Assistance; 15 lived alone in furnished rooms, and 7 lived alone in apartments.

There were 26 who came from foreign countries other than Great Britain.

The religious denominations were: 15 Protestants, 3 Catholics, and 22 Jews.

The work histories were divided as follows:

Skilled and unskilled labor—21 men. White collar and small business—6 men. Of the women, 8 had been housewives, 2 had done domestic service, 1 had been a clerk, and 2 had been factory workers.

40 MEMBERS:

MEN: 27   WOMEN: 13

Average Age: 71.8 Years

	MEN	WOMEN	TOTAL
Marital Status			
Married	12	3	15
Widowed	14	6	20
Single	1	4	5
Religious Background			
Protestant	7	8	15
Catholic	3	0	3
Jewish	17	5	22
National Origin			
American	3	6	9
Great Britain	4	1	5
Other European Countries	20	6	26

	MEN	WOMEN	TOTAL
Living Arrangements			
Apartment Alone	2	5	7
Furnished Room	12	3	15
With Spouse	11	4	15
With Children	2	1	3
Source of Income			
Old Age Assistance	22	13	35
Social Security + Savings	3	0	3
Relatives	2	0	2
Previous Occupation			
Skilled Labor	14	0	14
Unskilled Labor	7	0	7
White Collar	1	0	1
Small Business	5	0	5
Housewives	0	8	8
Domestic Service	0	2	2
Clerk	0	1	1
Factory Worker	0	2	2

We quote from the worker's records of her first fortnight.

On the first day there were 27 men and 3 women in the club. The men were playing cards and dominoes, three were reading newspapers, several sat by themselves doing nothing. Miss Hardy prepared coffee at 2 o'clock, and ordered the men to form a line for each to receive his coffee and cookies, after which they resumed their games.

When worker introduced herself to Miss Hardy she sensed a feeling of resentment in Miss Hardy's inquiry as to why she had been sent. The worker explained that she hoped to organize a program and stimulate interest in various activities. Miss Hardy answered that they were getting on very well under the present arrangement and that the men were only interested in card games. She showed the work the women were doing: patchwork, quilts, doilies and rugs.

The worker asked why so few women attended, and Miss Hardy said, "The girls usually come on Wednesdays." She told the worker at once that she would have difficulties with certain members, namely, Mr. Mann and Mr. Sacks.

She introduced the worker to Mr. Lowden, who had been helping with serving coffee. The worker told him of her plans and he offered to cooperate in every way but thought that while some of the men might be interested in more varied activities, most of them were not of the "mental calibre" to accept much stimulation.

She also met Mr. Halber who had taken on the jobs of dishwashing, cleaning, sweeping, etc. He complained that the other men did not help, that their only interest was in cards.

The worker circulated among the game tables and spoke to the players and to some of those sitting alone. Several expressed interest in seeing new activities started. One said he would like a Jewish newspaper; another said he just liked sitting and watching people coming in and out.

The worker was struck by several things on that first day. It was clear that Miss Hardy had taken over the management of the group, had determined how and when the refreshments were to be served, what work the women were to do, and when. But what puzzled her was the apparently complete acquiescence of the members in that management, and the passive and subdued attitude of most of them. Only two of the men took any part in the daily tasks of the club, and while the women listened to her, none of them made any comment on what she said. She was aware of Miss Hardy's negative attitude toward herself as newcomer and also her feeling that the status quo was satisfactory. She considered it all that could be expected of these people. As if to discourage any thought of change, Miss Hardy had singled out two problem members as samples of the impossibility of doing any more than she had done.

5/3. This day there were 12 women and 31 men present.
The worker again circulated among the women who all
seemed interested in her explanation of why she was at the
center, but again made no comments. Mrs. Mishkin, however, said she was glad the worker had come since she herself
was interested in "mental relaxation and recreation and not
merely work." The women looked at each other and threw
scornful glances at Mrs. Mishkin.

At 1:30 Miss Hardy arrived laden with packages and puff-
ing. She immediately told the worker how tired she was and
how difficult she finds carrying packages. The worker suggested the job was too hard for one person and should be
shared by all members of the center. Miss Hardy said she
would not be able to come again for some time as she had
many household duties and needed a rest. She immediately
started to prepare coffee. When the worker suggested that the
refreshments be served in the middle of the afternoon, Miss
Hardy said the members preferred to have them soon after
arrival and then "my girls can get to work." When Mr. Sacks
seemed to be in a hurry to get his coffee she scolded him. He
was offended and refused to take any refreshment.

After the serving Miss Hardy assigned doilies to be em-
broidered to the women and prepared the stand for the
patch-work quilt. Mrs. Badner, with an air of defiance, said
she preferred to do her own crocheting.

At 4 o'clock Miss Hardy handed the worker the keys of the
supply closet, holding them out at arm's length with an air
of hostile surrender. She explained what supplies she bought
and where, and added that she was certain the worker would
find it difficult to get the members to cooperate in these
chores. The worker again praised her for the fine work she
had done, urged her to come when she could, and said the
group would miss her.

The next day the worker had to leave for a short while
during the afternoon, and since this was the first day Miss
Hardy was not present, she asked several of the women, as
well as Mr. Lowden and Mr. Halber, whether they could
take over the serving of the refreshments. They assured her
they could. When she returned an hour later she found that
the women had served and cleaned up, and they seemed

pleased at her comment on how quickly and efficiently everything had been done.

Mr. Lowden told the worker that Mr. Isaacs, the oldest member of the club, would be 86 on the seventh of this month. The worker asked him and several of the other men whether they would not like to send him a birthday card. They were delighted with the idea and the worker promised to bring one. Mr. Lowden explained that on the next day, a Friday, he usually cannot come since it is his day for housecleaning. Mr. Lowden is a widower.

5/5. The worker was greeted very warmly and asked if she had brought the card. It was passed around and admired. Mr. Lowden then brought it back to the worker with Mr. Isaacs' home address so that she might mail it. She suggested that a member write the message and address since it was being sent by them. The women said Mr. Lowden should do so because of his fine handwriting. He asked them what message he should write. When no one offered a suggestion the worker offered several, but Mr. Lowden said he would like to write, "From the Happy Family of the Recreation Center." The ladies wholeheartedly approved of this. At the time there was only one other man present, so worker asked whether they should wait to see if some of the other men would like to share in the discussion. Mr. Lowden, however, told her, "These men do not understand such things." He wrote the card and added a note urging Mr. Isaacs to come to the center on a specific day. Mr. Lowden was asked by several members how he managed to be present on a Friday, and he said he had finished his housework quickly in order not to miss even one day's attendance.

The worker now asked the women whether they wished to resume the handwork which they had started and several assented. But she noticed that Miss Titchner seemed to hesitate and quickly told her she was only to do handwork if she wanted to. She saw that this statement surprised them. She therefore spoke of the purpose of the center, namely, that it was for companionship and enjoyment. She said that to some chatting and doing handwork at the same time was pleasant. At this they said frankly that they thought they must do handwork for sale in order to help pay for the refreshments.

The worker assured them that funds for this purpose would be available and that all handwork was to be done only if the doer enjoyed it.

A few days later, to make sure they believed her, she suggested at "work time" that they let it go and "let's just talk today." Two of the women offered to help in serving the refreshments. The worker poured coffee while Mr. Lowden helped with the sugar, cream, and cake. Mrs. Mishkin prepared to go immediately afterward, saying she was restless. The worker introduced her to Mr. and Mrs. Wimpel, who are members of a club in a nearby settlement house. She spent the rest of the afternoon with them, and then told the worker she enjoyed meeting them.

While the women were clearing the dishes they discussed a suggestion made by Miss Hardy before leaving, that they discontinue visiting the center and meet at her home instead. Since no one mentioned this directly to the worker, she made no comment.

5/8.   The worker found most of the members already in the lounge when she arrived at one o'clock. Many asked eagerly if Mr. Isaacs had received his card, and whether he was coming. The men were playing games, the women chatting together, but sitting as always in a group apart from the men. They now told her of Miss Hardy's plan that they leave the center and meet at her and each other's homes, and asked her opinion. The worker asked them how they felt about it and they all disapproved of this suggestion, saying they preferred to come to the center.

Another staff member of the Department of Welfare presently arrived bringing a birthday cake decorated with candles. The women offered to help with the refreshments. At 3 o'clock Mr. Lowden played the "Happy Birthday" tune on the piano, and all the members joined in the singing. Mr. John presented the cake to Mr. Isaacs, who was very pleased and thanked the group for this expression of their friendship. He then sang a ballad. The atmosphere became gay and hilarious and even the solitary Mr. Goldman joined in the fun. Refreshments were then served and many of the men commented on how much more relaxed they felt and how they had enjoyed the singing.

When the women were clearing the dishes, Mrs. Mishkin joined them to help. But Mrs. Douglas did not like her way of arranging them and said so sharply. Mrs. Mishkin complained to the worker and to Mrs. Seaman that she had been insulted. Mrs. Douglas was upset and said she would have to leave the center because of Mrs. Mishkin. The worker took her aside and tried to make her understand Mrs. Mishkin's feelings toward the group. She said that Mrs. Mishkin had not realized that there was a preferred way of doing this job, that this was her first attempt to help, that she was very sensitive, and in fact took correction as personal criticism. Mrs. Douglas said she understood, but nevertheless Mrs. Mishkin should not insist on doing things her way the first time she volunteered to help the others. However, she quickly recovered from her upset.

After Mrs. Douglas had left, the worker spoke to Mrs. Mishkin, who sobbed as she related her difficulties with the other women and pointed out how well she had got on with the couple to whom the worker had introduced her the day before. She said she planned to visit their club with them in the hope of finding congenial people there whom she could persuade to come to the center and thus protect herself from those women who had not accepted her.

When the worker rejoined the group several commented on Mr. Halber's absence, and Mr. Lowden offered to visit him to see if he were ill. Mrs. Weinburg came for the first time and timidly asked permission to use the sewing machine. The worker urged her to come at all times in order to use the facilities of the center.

Since Mr. Halber was still absent and he had attended to bringing water and other tasks, the worker spoke to several men to ask their help and each made some small contribution to the preparations. The women again did not volunteer to help and the worker made the coffee. They did, however, offer to do the clearing up.

The worker now discussed with them the possibility of forming a refreshment committee so that this service might be taken care of in case she should ever not be there. The women agreed that it should be their job but were afraid that none of them could do it adequately. The worker tried to reassure them. She then told several small groups that she was

planning to have a general meeting to discuss many of the
problems of the center and how all could help to organize it
into a club in which each could feel he was making his
contribution.

This meeting was held the next week, but in the first fifteen days of the worker's presence at the center certain important changes had taken place.

The members quickly sensed the difference between the
new worker's approach to them and that of Miss Hardy. The
latter had made all decisions about the club herself and enforced them. She had been patronizing toward the women
and distrustful and even hostile toward the men. The worker
had counteracted such attitudes at every opportunity. She
had expressed confidence in the group's willingness to cooperate and evinced a cordial and sensitive interest in each
individual. By unhurried stages she had managed to convert
the refreshment time into the social gathering it was meant
to be, seating the men and momen at the tables and serving
them as hostess. Though the women had received her first
little talks in silence, they now began to make significant
comments on "how much more relaxed and happier things
are" until finally one said, "It made me feel bad to see the
men queued up like a bread line."

The worker had waited until once in her absence the
women had accomplished the preparation, serving, and
clearing of the refreshments before suggesting that they take
over this task, and then discovered that their hesitation in
doing so was not due to unwillingness but to a fear of not
being competent to manage it by themselves.

These first days offered several opportunities for drawing
the group together. One was the news item of the oldest
member's approaching birthday which she could convert into
a group celebration in which every one participated. In preparing for it she made sure that even so small an act as

addressing the card and selecting the message be done by the members and not by her.

She made use of an indication of reluctance about "the girls getting to work" to open up new vistas of the club's purposes in which the emphasis was wholly on their wishes and enjoyment.

She also noted individual attitudes which were creating difficulties and tried to help these members to a greater acceptance by the group. Mrs. Mishkin was obviously rejected by the others, keenly aware of the fact, and trying to compensate by her feeling of intellectual superiority. She, therefore, provided her with new contacts, and when Mrs. Mishkin made her first and unsuccessful attempt to work with the other women, and the feeling against her came out into the open, the worker mediated between Mrs. Mishkin and her critic. Her explanation of the reasons for Mrs. Mishkin's reactions was a beginning of the long process, continuing today, of discussing the need and the ways of accommodating to each other's differences for the sake of the entire group.

Mr. Halber, who did the sweeping and general cleaning, likewise had a mistrust of others which conflicted with the capacity for leadership that his self-imposed activities indicated. While he was absent because of an injury to his hand, the worker made use of the opportunity to involve other men in cooperation on these tasks. On his return, she asked him if he was sure that this work would not be bad for his hand. He showed much pleasure at her concern. Perhaps it was this personal interest which made him willing to concede that his suspicions of the members might be unfounded. He had seen a newcomer peering into the kitchen, but agreed that he had not seen either him or the others actually take anything as he had suspected them of doing.

Each of these steps may seem slight, but attitudes and influence are conveyed and affirmed in just such small ways. They set the tone and the atmosphere in which a group is induced to function as a group. In those first two weeks the worker had found many ways of combining understanding and attention to individuals with consistently asking the group to make decisions and to assist in their group responsibilities.

We now include a record of the first membership meeting because of the contrast which it shows with the members as she found them, and because the meeting itself was an innovation which might be called the formal beginning of transforming this collection of individuals into a group which became aware of common aims, purposes, and shared interests.

At two o'clock the worker began to arrange the chairs in preparation for the meeting. All the men helped. Promptly at two-thirty the meeting began. After making a few introductory remarks the worker spoke of the purpose of the meeting. The group nodded its approval. Mr. Schultz rose to say that the purpose of the center was recreation, relaxation and companionship. Mr. Kraus asked for the floor and repeated his daily comment about the work he does in cleaning the center. The worker thanked him as she saw the other men snickering. She then spoke of such daily chores, stressing that no one was compelled to work but that in order to be comfortable, there were certain things which had to be done. For instance, if no one opened the windows, they would all suffer, or if the dishes were not washed, there would be none to use the next day. The members laughed heartily. There was applause from the floor indicating agreement that they all cooperate in performing the small tasks which would make the group comfortable, and that they wanted to be helpful.

She then asked them what were the things they liked about the center. Mr. Graber, who had not caught the question, said he would like a good radio. Someone else corrected his misunderstanding and then said he liked the friendliness. Mr. Graber said there was not enough friendliness and that people sometimes insulted each other. The worker spoke of the differences among people and the need to understand each other and to compromise. Again there seemed general approval.

She then asked what were some of the things they would like to have added to the program, saying that if she knew what things interested them, they might discuss how to include them. Again there was a request for a radio and Mr. Lowden said he had heard that a good one was being sent from Connecticut. Another asked for entertainment. When the worker inquired what they meant by entertainment, Mr. Blau said he would enjoy a good lecture. Mr. Bognor said he thought a rabbi should come to speak on racial tolerance. Some said they would like concerts or little shows. There was lively discussion and all agreed they wanted some outside interest at least once a week. Further suggestions came rapidly. They asked for cards, checkers, music, movies. One man suggested something more active, like ball. When the worker asked how many men would like to play ball, there was much laughter and most of them said that they were past ball days. She suggested shuffleboard. Mr. Veendorp thought this was a good game for old men. She suggested that the men plan to build a shuffleboard with sticks and discs.

She then spoke of crafts, enumerating many different kinds and told them that she could get materials if they were interested. Mr. Weinberg asked about war work and was told that some picture puzzles were available to assemble for use in the veterans' hospitals. Many said they would be glad to participate in this.

The worker now suggested that they plan a weekly schedule with different events each day and there was lively approval. They suggested that membership meetings be held on Mondays, since most of the women were present on that day and that Wednesdays and Fridays be reserved for crafts when the attendance of both men and women was good. Tuesdays and Thursdays might then be the days for musical programs or lectures. There was much interest in this discussion of a plan for the week. The worker pointed out that it might take time to get all these plans under way, but a member answered that, though securing outside entertainment might proceed slowly in the summer time, if it were started now, by fall things would be running smoothly.

The worker then told the membership that at the next

meeting they would elect officers and discuss plans for a Memorial Day observance. But Mr. Schultz arose and suggested that a president be elected at this meeting. She therefore asked for nominations. A lag occurred and then someone nominated her for president. The worker said that she was honored by their suggestion but that she was not eligible since only those past sixty years of age, i.e., members, could assume office. She thought that this slightly humorous reference to her own age would be an indirect way of stressing the difference in her role and theirs, but they took it seriously, as though the age rule of membership were the only distinguishing difference between their functions. Since some of them had not even caught this reasoning, she was again nominated for the office of vice-president, and then said more directly that only members should be chosen.

After this Mr. Schultz, who had clearly appreciated the point of self-government, nominated Mr. Lowden. All seemed to be in favor of having Mr. Lowden elected unanimously.

The next officer suggested was vice-president. Mr. Halber and Mr. Veendorp were nominated. Mr. Halber withdrew in favor of Mr. Veendorp. Since few women were present, the worker suggested they wait for the next meeting to complete nominations and that Mr. Lowden take over the chair. He spoke briefly of his appreciation of the election and his eagerness to do things for the club. The worker noted that he addressed the group as brothers and sisters. He said the worker was his boss and that they would work well together.

Meantime an official of the Department had arrived and the worker asked him to address the group. He congratulated Mr. Lowden on his presidency and thought the choice an excellent one. He added that he wished, however, to correct his statement that the worker was his boss. Mr. Lowden drew himself up and indignantly denied having said so. The visitor added pacifically that there were no bosses, but if any, the members would be the worker's boss. This was accepted good-humoredly.

He then talked to the group about the Russian experiment with the aged. He indicated that death at seventy years was a disease and that an important factor in longevity was happiness. The members clung to every word, even those who had difficulty in hearing or following the points.

After the talk Mr. Lowden announced that at the next meeting the elections would be completed and plans made for Memorial Day. He then adjourned the session.

The women busied themselves with the refreshments. Everyone stood around talking about the meeting. Several came over to ask the worker to repeat what the official had said and to explain to them what it meant. Some said they had heard something of this before and were very much interested.

Refreshments were served. Mrs. R. poured the coffee, Mrs. W. poured the tea. Mr. Renziti introduced himself to the worker and told her that he was a skilled carpenter who had made many of the fixtures at the center. He had been away due to illness, but would be pleased to help as soon as he was well enough. She asked him if he knew how to build a shuffleboard and he thought he could if he saw a model or a picture.

After refreshments were served and dishes cleared, everyone sat around chatting. They commented that the afternoon had gone very quickly and that they did not realize that it was time to go home to prepare for the evening meal. The worker heard several say that they were looking forward to the next meeting because this one had been so enjoyable.

In her contact with the members in the previous two weeks the worker had laid the ground work for the topics which she introduced at the meeting. One was the need for cooperation in the maintenance chores of the club, which she could now present as a matter for their joint consideration. This was the final step in changing the type of leadership they had had—from the former dictatorial control to voluntary cooperation focused on one of the most obvious services to the club.

The other topics were expanded activities and the suggestion that the club institute an organization of self-government with elected officers.

What is striking about the record is the responsiveness and initiative of the group at this first opportunity to take a hand in shaping their club. There were many suggestions for occupations and a lively interest in planning a schedule for the week. That there were interests beyond those already offered was evidenced by the discussion on special events, music, shows, lectures; and by a lucky chance they were given a brief talk on the subject of old age, with the concept that interests and activity could do much to prevent deterioration.

This topic, so central to their interests, was to be continued throughout the years, both in talks by the worker, by invited speakers, and in many private conferences. As it was elaborated, it provided new perspectives on their problems and attitudes and was one of the main topics of a continuous process of group education—one to which we will often refer.

At this meeting the women still sat segregated at the rear of the room, but the worker's careful inclusion of them in each discussion led them to move into the meeting physically as well as to participate actively. From this time on they assumed charge of the refreshments.

We will save for its own chapter the evolution of self-government, but here again there was prompt response as though the new climate of the club was releasing an initiative which had been latent and only waiting for opportunity and stimulation.

Perhaps it will be objected that all the steps and results which are here recorded are the commonplaces of social group work, as indeed they are. Yet it has been our experience in the past years with students and others trained in group work with other age levels, to find them slow to realize that these same methods apply to groups of older people. While the first worker assumed that these were the methods to use, she nevertheless was uncertain as to their probable results because of the special characteristics of these clients, namely, their self-absorption, their general insecurity, a frequent tendency to hostility and suspicion, and a conspicuous lack of ease in being together. But her insight into the meaning of these symptoms grew as the members showed growth and development in their new setting. Both staff and members were the products of a culture which hitherto had set little value on the later years. If the staff had at first little knowledge of what might be expected of the older person, so had the clients little hope of a change in their dreary lot and even less expectation that given new opportunities, encouragement, guidance and teaching, they would again discover in themselves abilities and interests which could grow and develop.

CHAPTER THREE

Self-Government

This much of the first records will suffice to give an early picture of these old people in action and the stir of liveliness and change that came in response to leadership. The suggestion that they set up a self-government organization with the election of officers was a plan by which the worker hoped, in furnishing a formal procedure, to further capture and develop their participation. To many of the men who had formerly belonged to unions and lodges this was a familiar institution. The worker was also aware that the prestige of being elected to office would afford additional means of securing status for these older people who needed it so much.

At this time membership meetings were still held weekly and she proposed that they consider introducing self-government and discuss it at the next meeting. We have already reported how this suggestion was taken up at once by Mr. Schultz and how Mr. Lowden and Mr. Veendorp were then unanimously elected to the offices of president and vice-president.

At the next meeting, a week later, the same confusion in regard to the functions of staff and members was again revealed and she was nominated for the office of secretary. Again she explained, as simply as possible, the purpose of these offices; namely, that they themselves, through their elected representatives, would conduct the affairs of the center. Since this responsibility seemed to alarm them, she assured them that she would be glad to help at all times. Such repeated confusion and necessary explanations could not occur today but were typical of these first members. Mr. Halber was then elected secretary, again unanimously.

These three men had been known to the others because of their assertive behavior from the time the group was first gathered together. At this stage assertiveness was a quality which stood out against the timidity of most members and made them almost inevitable choices.

Since the institution of self-government has, over the years, been the area which has most clearly reflected the growth and changes in attitude of the membership, we should like to report in some detail about the personalities and the functioning of these first officers in contrast with those who were to be chosen later.

Mr. Lowden was a man about whose life the worker obtained information from the Department of Welfare records, as well as much direct information throughout his subsequent years at the center. He was then 70 years of age, slender and erect, with finely modeled features. He walked with a rigid gait, had poor vision, and a tight, unhappy expression. This same rigidity was reflected in all his behavior. He had always been dominated, first by his parents and then by his wife, and at this time, when he was a widower, by his late wife's cousin who was his landlady. His subsequent exaggerated self-assertion and dictatorial attitude at the center therefore seemed to be a compensation for his previous submissiveness. In later years, long after his presidency, whenever there was any disturbance in the lounge, he would confide to a staff member that when he was president he used an iron hand to keep order and such things didn't happen! Coupled with this rigidity was a constant tension which suggested great insecurity. His relationships to others at the center were not genuinely warm and personal, though he had a daily ritual of shaking hands with each one and calling them by their first names.

He presided at membership meetings with great dignity and much use of the gavel to enforce absolute silence, but with little tolerance of any members who wished to speak during discussions. A half-hour meeting was the maximum he could stand and after that he would become restless and impatient to bring it to a close.

He was resistant to forming an executive committee, but when the purpose and value of such a body was reviewed, said he understood and wished personally to select its members. He omitted anyone who showed potential leadership qualities and selected instead those who were certain to agree with him. The worker discussed and explained democratic procedure over and over again, but whenever he was not in complete agreement with her he would threaten to resign, only to come back the next day to say that he had not been feeling well and that he hoped no one had taken him seriously. At executive meetings he took little part, leaving that responsibility to the vice-president.

A member suggested that the term of office run for six months and the others, who were still quite apathetic about such decisions, agreed. But Mr. Lowden resented this member quite openly for thus limiting the tenure of office.

Mr. Veendorp, as vice-president, had no understanding of his role nor its responsibilities, although he enjoyed the prestige of holding that title. He was a short, choleric Dutchman whose boisterous manner at games and willingness to help when called upon had made him known to the members. He knew that he was to take Mr. Lowden's place in the event of his absence, but on the one occasion when the latter was late and a speaker was to be introduced, he hastily persuaded Mr. Wyman to take his place, explaining to the worker that Mr. Wyman's English was better. As the members became more experienced in conducting meetings, they began to be critical of his inadequate performance and lack of responsibility, and commented that he preferred to go home to listen to ball games rather than to attend a meeting. At the following election he resigned.

Mr. Halber as secretary could read and write English, but he was so nervous that he could barely manage to read the minutes. It was such a relief to him when he finished that he failed to note the subsequent developments of that meeting. He had a notebook but preferred to jot down his records on scraps of paper which he was always going to copy into the

notebook but never did. Consequently the worker always had
to help him prepare the minutes after each meeting.

But at executive meetings at which the officers prepared
the agenda for the membership meetings, he was most active,
generally suggesting that discussions be held on the care of
the center and volunteering to speak on these matters at the
membership meeting.

After a visit to a local hospital where he delivered some
bags made by the members, he gave an excellent report. He
had been frightened before giving it and needed much reassurance from the worker but was very satisfied with its success.

Although he had previously been active as handyman at
the center and in this role was exacting and suspicious if
others used tools and misplaced them, this new activity
seemed to afford him great satisfaction. His previous quarrelsome relations with his landlady improved, both because he
was away most of the day and because he had so much satisfaction in telling her of his center activities.

As the second election drew near Mr. Freeman made a motion that the terms of office be extended to one year, since
half a year was barely enough time for officers to learn their
duties. This was passed.

Mr. Lowden, who was obviously much concerned whether
he would again be nominated, began telling members he
would refuse if it happened. Mr. Weinberg therefore prepared himself for nomination as he had been active in meetings and made many suggestions. However, Mr. Lowden was
nominated and accepted readily. Mr. Weinberg declined
either to run against him or be nominated for any other
office. He continued to serve on the executive committee
despite the fact that Mr. Lowden was not eager to have him.

The secretary this time was a Mr. Stengel, aged 71, a man
who had impressed the others as intelligent since he read the
newspapers diligently and discussed politics. He had poor
eyesight and a facial deformity, which, combined with his
great tension and difficulty in reading, made him almost
unintelligible. He too found it hard to take notes of the proceedings, and between his poor performance and Mr. Lowden's critical attitude toward him, became so discouraged
that he told the worker he wished to resign. She pointed out
that he had been improving, helped him with suggestions for

the minutes, and typed them in large print so that he did better. However, the end of his term of office came as a relief to him; yet he continued to take other responsibilities such as the daily locking of windows and closets.

Mr. Schultz was made vice-president. He was then 71, a widower, of German birth, with better schooling than most of the members. He was a quiet, poised person, who accepted office willingly and thoroughly understood his role. Though he never had the opportunity of presiding at membership meetings he was always active in making reports and stimulating interest in center affairs.

He was to respond to the opportunities which the center offered with an excellent balance between his own interests and needs and service to the community, and with insight and understanding of the needs and often the shortcomings and foibles of others.

In the face of Mr. Lowden's tenacity in holding the center of the stage, it needed considerable adroit maneuvering to help Mr. Schultz to reach the position and roles he was so capable of filling. For instance, as birthday parties became a regular feature he assisted in planning the program and presided. The worker made this possible by persuading Mr. Lowden that if he could be relieved of this responsibility, he could then be among the guests of honor. Mr. Schultz's management of this party was excellent and many members praised his performance.

At executive meetings he presided and quickly advanced from needing the worker's help to an efficient independence of any assistance. Once at an executive meeting which he did not attend, they planned a special celebration and appointed him master of ceremonies. He was most willing. On the day of the celebration, however, Mr. Lowden insisted on presiding and Mr. Schultz agreed without discussion, explaining to the worker that it meant much to Mr. Lowden but not to him. He showed this same understanding of Mr. Lowden a year later when he himself was nominated for the office of president and declined the nomination, saying that it meant too much to Mr. Lowden for him to deprive him of office. He well understood the value of rotation of officers, but was content to wait until the membership as a whole had achieved greater independence of judgment and could assert their wishes for more democratic representatives.

Two years after the beginning of self-government, Mr. Sullivan suggested before the nominations that a special meeting be held for this purpose. There was active discussion by the members regarding the duties of officers. The worker also pointed out the need for more officers and they recommended adding a corresponding secretary and a sergeant-at-arms. They set a date for a nomination meeting and at this meeting chose an election committee and decided to have closed ballots. This was a great advance over the timid behavior of the early days. It represented greater know-how and a critical evaluation of their own experience as well as a strong collective interest in conducting the affairs of the center.

At this time a woman was chosen as corresponding secretary since she had shown her capability in answering letters. Mr. Lowden and Mr. Schultz were again elected to office, unopposed, but a new man, Mr. Edwards, was elected by an overwhelming majority to the office of recording secretary. The previous bad experience with secretaries who were barely able to write and who read poorly now made the group quick to recognize the superior abilities of this man and later to express approval of his efficiency and his articulate delivery of the minutes.

At this time the need for a constitution and by-laws was discussed. Mr. Edwards, who had eight years' experience as secretary of a sectarian society, came to the meeting with notes prepared to discuss the matter.

By means of the constitution the tenure of office had been limited to two years, and under this arrangement to date there have been six presidents in the nine years of the center's existence. Each incumbent's performance in office is of course primarily determined by his personality, his past experience in dealing with people, and his education. But holding office for two years is an experience which has developed leadership ability to a remarkable extent.

Membership meetings are now held monthly. They are always well attended, discussion from the floor is spontaneous and lively, and represents many viewpoints. Therefore, an officer is subjected to constant reactions of approval or criticism, and his task of reconciling viewpoints and of holding a representative balance calls for skill and good judgment with people.

An illustration of such development in office is afforded by the third president, Mr. Mannheim. He had come to the center some two years before his nomination, and though he made exploratory visits to some of the special activities, was not interested in joining any of them. He was then 73 years old, a tall, slender man, formerly a shoemaker by trade. He had an easy manner and a pleasant smile. He speaks English with a strong Jewish accent and a limited vocabulary. When he first came to the center, he had two sources of security which contrasted with most of the other members. He had excellent relationships with his children and grandchildren, and at that time still had money of his own. He therefore had not suffered the sense of defeat which others had experienced due to long years of isolation and because of receiving public assistance. He quickly made friends among many of the card players and was popular with the women.

When he was elected, he took great pride in this distinction, but his limited ability to deal with discussion or opposition was patent. His manner was crude ("Who said you could talk? Sit down!"), yet this soon proved to be more a lack of polish than a drive for self-assertion. He had great personal security and therefore a flexibility in understanding and in tolerating differences—a flexibility which became clearer as he quickly learned more acceptable forms of speech and techniques of conducting meetings from the worker's example.

He also felt a personal responsibility toward newcomers in welcoming them to the center and stressing "Here you can be happy mitout we think of your race or color; it is here a real democracy!" He took over responsibilities for the daily management of the center. As the problem of caring for hats and coats became urgent, he helped build partitions in the cloak room and made hat checks out of the tops of Dixie cups. When finally cloak-room clerks and cleaners were secured, he made sure that furniture was moved and kitchen corners and window sills thoroughly scrubbed.

When a retired barber came to the center, there was much discussion about having him offer a hair-cutting service to the members. This involved arranging for renewal of his license, towel service, supplies, a chair, tools, etc., and took some time. Mr. Mannheim became impatient and finally took action by discussing the matter with the president of the Board of Directors, explaining that as the two presidents who managed the center, they must push this matter through.

At the end of Mr. Mannheim's first year in office, he came to the staff for data on the amounts of supplies used in refreshments and other statistics concerning the center, which he used in a report of his year in office. This was an innovation not followed by later presidents, but typical of his attitude while in office—that of a practical stewardship of center affairs.

During his two years in office he became much attached to one of the women members and visited her daily. But he could not bring himself to decide on marriage because of his poor health, because his children were opposed, and finally because his savings were being steadily exhausted.

The end of his presidency coincided with the end of his financial resources and he had to apply for Old Age Assistance. This must have been a difficult adaptation because Mr. Mannheim formerly took great pleasure in standing treats of ice cream or candy to his particular group of friends. However, he made this adjustment in dignified silence.

Later his woman friend suddenly married someone else. This event required a more severe readjustment and he looked ill and wretched for some weeks. But today he has adjusted to this disappointment also. He has found a new activity in the discussion group of Current Events. Here his sound common sense and balanced viewpoint give him renewed status. He also serves on the executive committee, as do all former officers, as well as being chairman of the visiting committee.

With the next president, vice-president and sergeant-at-arms, a wholly new development occurred, namely, a strong trend against staff "interference." The circumstances under which it began, as well as the comments of many of the members, indicate that it was mainly confined to the three officers in question, but it became vocal in connection with a change in the income allowance of those on Old Age Assistance, a matter which affected over ninety per cent of the membership. In meetings both the vice-president and the sergeant-at-arms frequently began to say, "We can manage our own affairs and the staff is here only to attend to office work." Since this trend superficially seemed to combine both potentially good features of greater self-reliance with a confusion and even resentment about the role of staff, we believe that this was a development which may be of interest to report for the benefit of other workers.

The next election came just at a time when the Department of Welfare reduced the budgets of those receiving Old Age Assistance. This caused tremendous anxiety and upset in all the recipients and was one of the occasions when the mood of the lounge reflected a mass contagion of worry, a sense of helplessness and resentment. Few recipients understood the complex computations between federal, state and municipal contributions to Old Age Assistance grants, nor the machinery by which changes in the cost-of-living index cause new budget adjustments. A meeting was called and the headworker explained these matters in detail, and also promised to discuss as many of the individual budgets as possible. At this time a local newspaper conducted a campaign against this cut, interviewing sample recipients to prove that the reduction caused hardship. This publicity greatly added to the disturbance at the center.

The new president, Mr. Stahl, then 60-odd, was an American-born Jew, a former shoe salesman, who could not work because of a heart condition, and who had come to the center some months before. He was a personable man, well-groomed, with high color and youthful appearance despite his white hair. He had become known to the members because of his

performance in a recent dramatics club play—and perhaps
represented a compromise choice between the foreign-born
Jewish members and those who had begun to murmur about
having a representative "who speaks English," meaning without foreign accent.

His team-mate, Mr. Falk, the vice-president, was also an
American-born Jew. He was a compact, capable, aggressive
man, aged 75, whose heart condition likewise had forced him
to retire, though he looked and seemed young and energetic.

Mr. Falk had been active in politics all his life, as a worker
in local party organizations, and at the center constantly
referred to all the influential people he knew. When he had
been nominated as sergeant-at-arms the year before, he had
made a vehement campaign speech about law and order, and
the discipline he would enforce if elected. He was elected and
proceeded as he had promised, stirring up considerable resentment by his harsh methods. Not long after this he had a
heart attack which kept him in the hospital and at home for
several weeks. Mr. Falk often refers to this attack as "the time
when my job here landed me in the hospital."

In his absence Mr. Wilman agreed to finish out his term of
office and was then himself elected as sergeant-at-arms, and
Mr. Falk became vice-president.

During the period of the new budget cuts Mr. Falk rose
during a birthday party program to make an inflammatory
speech about the reduced allowances, claiming that they were
due to the new political administration against whose election he had warned the membership. He said that although
he himself was not a recipient he was "spending his life's
blood" to work with those who would undo this hardship.
The suggestion of a corrupt administration responsible for
their budget reductions and the intimation that he knew
influential people who could change these cuts was agitating
and confusing to the already upset membership.

The worker on duty reminded him that this was a birthday
program and that his speech was out of order, but that he
could address the members at another time on this matter.

He was acutely resentful and called the lounge to attention the next day. He said that the staff was allied with the Department of Welfare and therefore unwilling to have the members' "good and welfare" discussed. He added that the members could run their own affairs, and need take no interference from staff. After this meeting there was much discussion in sub-groups about his attitude. Some were only concerned about the suggestion of help through political influence, but others were resentful about his attitude toward staff. Most of such members had had longer experience than he of the role of staff, either as guiding and facilitating the activities of special groups, or as counselors to those with personal problems. A few said explicitly that if it were not for the mediating influence of staff "everybody in this place would be at each other's throats." Mr. Falk himself took part in only one special interest, a discussion group, and has never asked for any special counseling help. His influence on the new president, Mr. Stahl, was great.

Mr. Stahl was a man of limited outlook and great insecurity. He has been twice married, once divorced, and then separated from his second wife. His grown children did not see him though they lived in the same city. He showed both great need of prestige and recognition, and also great vulnerability to group disapproval.

On one occasion he criticised a donated Christmas dinner, saying it was skimpy and inadequate. When the members disagreed violently, he flushed and left the room. At another time he insisted that a costume be rented for him for his song in the dramatics group play, although all the other members were content to be outfitted by efforts of the sewing group.

When he first presided as president he was nervous and insecure in procedure. The head worker sat nearby to prompt him, facilitate procedure, and smooth discussion, as had been her custom. But Mr. Falk, the vice-president, later told him she had no official right to do so and that she must ask for the floor before speaking. Mr. Stahl's inadequacy in conducting a meeting made him susceptible to this implication that his office was being ignored.

At the following meeting, when she again spoke in the informal manner which had been customary whenever the presiding officer seemed at a loss, he suddenly flushed with anger and slamming the gavel on the table, said that she must ask the chair's permission to speak and not treat him like a "dummy" or he would resign.

The members were startled by this sudden display of hostility and there was dead silence. The worker said slowly that he had been chosen by the majority and that he could not just give up this responsibility at will, that they depended on him, but that it took time to learn all that the office involved. She said that staff was here to help in this learning, as in all other matters which the members wished.

She briefly reviewed the history of self-government at the center, saying that they had started with only three officers, but that as the membership had grown the number of officers needed had doubled. She added that no one officer could be expected to do all the work involved in his office, but that part of his job was to delegate responsibility to others. Moreover, each new officer finds it difficult at first to recognize all the members who wish to speak, and in this, as in other ways, the staff's role is to assist him. In addition to helping with these responsibilities of his office, she pointed out that membership meetings are the only times when the staff can share with all the members the items of importance which have come up within the month. The length of her speech was deliberate, both to give feelings time to settle, and because several variations of a point are necessary to carry meaning to all. The background about self-government which she filled in, implied that the role of the officers was of increasing importance, and also conveyed to Mr. Stahl that all presidents went through a learning period, and that his was not, as the vice-president had made him feel, a sign of incompetence.

He therefore had time to recover his poise and to be molli-fied by her emphasis that the presidency was an honor be-stowed by the majority who would be unwilling to accept his resignation. But there were many currents of feeling when the meeting ended. Some members took his explosion as a sign of incompetence and openly said so. Others said tol-erantly, "He'll learn." Members who had been there a long time, and who regarded him as a relative newcomer, resented his attitude toward the head worker for whom they had a feeling of special affection due to their long and close rela-tionship to her.

There were three factors which precipitated the new dis-unity of group feeling in this meeting: a president insecure in his role of office, and, as was shown in other areas, very much in need of the personal reassurance which comes from feeling exceptional and outstanding; a vice-president who had experience and competence in political organizational work, but so far had not been able to use these assets to give himself a satisfying status at the center; and a factor external to the center but which caused an undercurrent of worry and help-lessness in the membership in regard to their subsistence standards.

The vice-president, Mr. Falk, found an outlet for his own dissatisfaction by playing on the president's unfamiliarity with parliamentary procedure to intimate that the staff was usurping his rights of office.

He thus precipitated Mr. Stahl into a sudden and severe conflict between his own need for prestige and his sense of inadequacy. The worker's speech helped him to resolve some of this conflict, and at the same time he again sensed, as once before, the reaction of the members, namely their disapproval of his outburst toward her. When the meeting ended, he came to the office to ask her if she were angry with him. She told him that, on the contrary, she felt the whole discussion had been profitable, that he had given her an opportunity to explain many things to the members, such as the function of the officers and the duties of the staff; that this was necessary and valuable to everyone, especially to the newcomers. She said she felt grateful to him for affording her the opportunity of making these matters clear.

This reassurance made it possible for him to come to her from time to time for the behind-the-scenes help in preparing the agenda which he needed. She in turn was punctilious in asking for the floor at meetings before commenting on any point.

This resulted in a modus vivendi for this president which lasted throughout his single term of office. But throughout this period his interest was mainly in the prestige of being president. He showed none of the sense of responsibility or stewardship which had characterized his predecessor. He learned to preside with confidence, but lacked the imagination to go beyond the role of figure-head, and when the next election time came, refused a second nomination.

While Mr. Stahl was still president, Mr. Falk's need for status shifted to the meetings of the executive committee in which the vice-president presides. Here he insisted that the previously informal discussions be conducted rigidly according to Robert's Rules, a copy of which he brought to the sessions.

The sense of competition with the staff which he had revealed so openly at the membership meeting he now transferred to these sessions. But in this more intimate group it was possible to bring this issue into the open and discuss with him more fully the role of the officers and the function of staff. The first few executive meetings became tense through his application of rules; his barking orders that no one was to speak before asking the chair's permission. These sessions had hitherto been informal affairs, around a table, where discussion flowed in an atmosphere of give and take. Now

Mr. Schultz, who felt Mr. Falk's hostility to the head worker behind these procedural restrictions, protested, saying they had always got along in the past without such methods and that they were unnecessary in so small a group. Since this intimated that Mr. Falk, a relative newcomer compared to Mr. Schultz, was being foolishly officious, it did nothing to modify his attitude.

The worker, however, sensed the frustrations behind his belligerence and had a private talk with him in which she frankly confronted him with the issue: did he think she was competing with him; did he think she wanted to be vice-president. This suddenly clarified the atmosphere as he conceded that was neither her wish nor her role. She then continued her explanation of their respective functions, which she repeated later to the whole executive committee. She likened self-government, the staff's function, and that of the Board of Directors' to the city, state and federal governments; the areas of responsibility of each; and the limitations of each. She explained, by examples, how each related to the other; where and how each could make recommendations for the others' policies, but that all had to work together. This gave an objective frame of reference for the power structure at the center, which together with her understanding of Mr. Falk's own needs, gradually abated his struggle to assert himself in destructive ways.

She realized, however, that behind his personal struggle for authority, albeit focused on the trappings of procedure, was a new development in membership attitudes. However much it was still confined to the symbols rather than the responsibility of office, this jealousy of "interference" was nevertheless a healthy sign. She therefore curbed her casually interjected comments, aware that this development must be given free play.

Later in the year a more cogent issue again brought the matter of membership control to the fore. There were two members whose behavior made them a storm center to the community; the one because his advancing senility made him increasingly objectionable; the other for similar reasons though his behavior was merely childish and impulsive. Several of the committee agreed with Mr. Falk that they should be debarred from the club and felt that the head worker's objections to this action was a negation of the committee's authority.

She explained her reasons with great care. In regard to the one man she pointed out that he was sick, not in body but in mind, indicating that provision for his case must come through the Department of Welfare and medical care. She was arranging this and was mentioning it to them in confidence. She likewise took them into her confidence about the other man, pointing out that he was not responsible for his actions, but that they were harmless, and he would be miserably lonely if debarred from the club since he had no other place to go.

Mr. Mannheim, who as former president was a member of the executive committee, warmly supported this point of view that the club should be tolerant of those who needed it so much and whose behavior might be silly but was inoffensive.

The committee and Mr. Falk were won over in this case. The discussion began a new weighing of behavior problems. Those who understood the purposes of the club, and who, like Schultz and Mannheim, understood the needs and foibles of certain members, could in the discussions of this representative committee, make their insight counterbalance the demands of those to whom control over membership had not included these implications of careful discrimination.

The discussions were a fruitful preparation for the responsibility which this committee presently assumed of taking disciplinary action. Being debarred from the center was modified to suspension for a week and was applied only after careful deliberation. So far it has been used only once, in the case of a woman whose persistent quarreling and troublemaking made it an appropriate and salutary step.

But this power, now so carefully exercised, is a new landmark of growth. The executive committee, because it has the advantages of a smaller group in which interaction is more potent and learning thereby accelerated, has achieved a sound independence of staff. If we seem to have digressed into this detailed account of the executive committee, it is because we followed the course of Mr. Falk's confused struggle against "staff interference" as it was transferred from membership meetings to this group's functioning. This committee is the essential body of the self-governing structure, and as Mr. Falk's struggle was resolved in this setting, it played its part in clarifying this group's understanding of their function and so advancing them to their present status.

We would now return to our account of the presidents in order to complete the picture of that portion of the self-governing organization.

In the next election three candidates were nominated for the presidency, of whom, for the first time, one was a woman. She was an American-born Italian, whose husband had been a member for some time. Young at 62, energetic and comely, with a real understanding of people and great ease in public speaking, her quick rise to a leadership role was not surprising. Opinions about her candidacy were sharply divided, especially among the women. Interestingly enough, a considerable number of those who had been in that early, self-effacing group, were most strongly in favor of electing her, while a few of the newcomers were shocked at the idea of having a woman for president. Her nomination, however, split the votes of the other two candidates, Mr. Falk and Mr. Schultz.

The pre-election time marked a new era at the center. All Mr. Falk's experience in ward politics came into play in campaigning. The two men were a complete contrast in personalities. Mr. Schultz was quiet and modest. He already had status at the center, and many sources of satisfaction through his diversified activities. Mr. Falk took occasional part in only one of the activities other than card playing. Holding office was his sole measure of success as well as the only kind of activity which interested him, and he campaigned with a drive which Mr. Schultz made no effort to match. Yet the vote was so close that he was elected by a majority of only two.

Once elected, he invited an official of the local political club to officiate at the installation ceremonies, and made a speech in which he promised to make this the finest club of its kind in the country.

Soon after he came to the office to say with unexpected frankness that he felt the staff had not wanted him to become president. He had sensed something behind their strictly noncommittal attitude throughout the campaigning, and was uneasy unless he could come to terms with it. The two workers with whom he spoke both said he was right and that they had real reservations about his candidacy. They recalled the intensity with which he had taken the duties of sergeant-at-arms, and his subsequent heart attack, and said that they felt he would think it necessary to be even more strenuous as president and be even more upset by the many conflicting viewpoints which he would have to face. The head worker added that she would always be glad to talk over such problems with him, and that they would work together.

He was tremendously reassured by this talk. The remaining traces of his former competition were replaced by an attitude of lavish praise for "our supervisors, God bless 'em." As he told us a little more about his past history we saw that this new term for staff workers dated back to the time when, as a small boy, he had been enrolled in a settlement house and gave us a clue to the conflict with authority which he must then have felt.

He has been in office two years. To him the role of president is not that of representing the wishes of the members but of being in authority over them and of building up his conception of what makes a club important. He decided that the membership meetings must open with reciting the oath of allegiance. Under the agenda item, "good and welfare," a term borrowed from lodge meetings, he generally speaks on membership behavior, giving examples of what will not be tolerated here, that it affects the reputation of the club, and how does it look to outsiders. He enforces brusquely the various rules which have gradually been introduced as membership increased.

But he has also changed. As his security and satisfaction in this role increased he has become more flexible, more friendly in his platform manner, and more understanding and tolerant toward others.

His second campaign for reelection was again against Mr. Schultz, and temporarily again upset these evidences of security. This time, however, he won by a larger majority. This was probably due to the changed membership, of whom a large number have come in the last few years. They do not know Mr. Schultz, nor the former tone of the club which he represents. Nor could he make himself felt by contrast with Mr. Falk. They, therefore, accept the latter as representative of this new environment since they know nothing of that atmosphere of more intimate participation, when the membership was not so large. Those who were part of that earlier period are keenly aware of the difference, but being in the minority, cannot counteract a trend compounded of such diverse elements of change.

Some of the elements of this change can be differentiated and account in part for this new tone which Mr. Falk represents. Mr. Lowden, the first president, was autocratic, but with a difference. His domination was an uncomplicated drive of his later years, which, by joining the center and becoming president, found an unexpected outlet. It was a simple self-assertion, not based on any previous experience with group organizations. Also, it was largely confined to the setting of presiding at meetings. It operated on a membership that had not yet acquired any strong group feeling such as today is represented by pride in the club. In addition, the individual members were timid and insecure. The prevailing tone was set by the staff and was permissive, accepting and continuously supportive of both officers and members, and that tone was the climate then necessary to and welcomed by the group.

Today the membership has a strong cohesiveness and great assurance about the club. They no longer need that former climate, and through their assurance, they, rather than the staff, set the tone in which control is acceptable and this kind of leadership represents strength. "He's a good president, he doesn't let people get away with anything." A corollary to acceptance of this brusque control is that they also feel they can afford to criticize him. In short, the atmosphere is tougher and that toughness reflects the fact that their tone is now dominant.

This does not mean that the staff is any less active in membership policy, but that the area of activity has shifted. Whereas formerly it had to be leadership in full view, it now functions behind the scenes in various ways. The staff must protect the individual from too harsh an impact of this control. In the case of the woman who was to be suspended for a week, the committee's decision was left to the head worker to enforce. This could then be done with a minimum of damage and interpreted in terms she understood and could accept.

At other times, as in the case of the childish member, the staff again could protect and support this rejected individual until such a time as the group itself modified its attitude toward him. It is also necessary to curb self-assertion at the expense of the group, or to help in channeling aggressiveness into constructive and acceptable outlets. In short, the mediating influence of staff is felt and even counted on, even though there is no longer a need that the staff be obviously active.

Before closing this chapter on the evolution of self-government as reflected through its officers, we must add the parallel changes in the membership during those nine years.

The greatest change in group performance which has come about in the last nine years can be seen in the monthly membership meetings. When we compare the assured procedure, the focused discussions and the close attention to these discussions with the insecure performance of former years, the contrast is striking. One of the most objective contrasts lies in the time element. Years ago a meeting which lasted an hour was invaded in the second half by restlessness. People began talking to each other and many left the room. Today a two hour meeting is not unusual and there is sustained attention throughout. We have therefore had to revise our idea that old people's span of attention is short, realizing that it lengthens as interest increases.

It is hard to evaluate the factors which are responsible for these changes. One is certainly experience, for some of the active participants today were among the first group and have learned what to do and how and what results to strive for. But this is more than mere experience in procedure. It is also experience of each other, of having come to know each other well through the years, and having established habits of working together.

Another factor is that in these later years of increasing membership there are many more adequate old people who have come than was formerly the case. This might seem to be merely the result of numbers—the larger attendance, the greater will be the number of competent individuals and the more their leadership will be felt. But it is also due to a wider knowledge in the community about such centers which comes to the ears of those who retire and who, therefore, come before any damage has occurred due to prolonged isolation. Certainly, the main factors are more competent leaders acting upon and reacting to a more experienced membership. This sets the tone of confidence in themselves—a confidence which undoubtedly in turn has its effect on newcomers.

The present officers, together with the leaders of various committees, take for granted their responsibility for initiating rules and policy and for presenting them for membership discussion, as well as seeing to it that, if accepted, they are enforced. In many cases they insisted on measures about which the staff had doubts, or felt they represented an authoritarian strictness which the staff shrank from applying. We asked ourselves whether this was not an example of the kind of permissive protectiveness which at first had been necessary and fruitful but which this enlarged and more competent membership had outgrown. It seemed so and thereby convicted us of not being as quick as the members to recognize a new stage of independence.

For instance, the gradual transition from a small group of members to a large attendance involved certain changes in practice which began to loom large as problems before the staff had clearly recognized their existence. We must digress a moment to give, as an example, the changes which took place in the manner of serving refreshments.

We remind the reader how the refreshment hour had been converted from the "bread line" to the sociable gathering it was meant to be. But we also realized that the refreshments were important as food. For most of the members living on minimal budgets the cup of coffee, the daily slice of cake, were welcome additions to the day's nourishment. Therefore, there were also, and increasingly, as attendance grew, explosions and accusations that some one had had more than his fair share. Here and there extra portions were pilfered, the left-over cake vanished into a knitting bag, a can of milk disappeared. At first we were inclined to balance the rarity of these occurrences against consideration of the need which prompted them and to take no action. But as the community became self-confident it became articulate about standards of behavior in this area as well as in others, and it became clear that portioning must be controlled. The indignation of the majority against the peculations of the few pointed up that anything less than strictness was inappropriate and unfair. Therefore, refreshment checks were introduced.

This watchfulness over the privileges and obligations of membership showed itself in many ways. Three years ago the members demanded membership cards. This seemed to be a wish to have a tangible token of belonging, and also a desire to be like the other organizations they had formerly known; i.e., unions and lodges. But presently qualifications for receiving the cards were suggested. No one should receive a card on the first day of arrival. There should be a kind of probationary period of one month from that date before they were issued. In that way "we can really know by the attendance records whether a person wants to come, not just issue cards to any one who drops in." Moreover, no one in that first month should come to the birthday party, but must wait out his month since admission should be by card only. This expressed the feeling that admission to that occasion was a privilege which should be confined to members only, and even more, to members whose participation in center affairs justified that admission. There are frequent and sharp comments on those who attend rarely and mainly on this day. "All they want is to come to a party. They never do anything for the center."

By this standard of value, namely, to give to the community in return for the benefits of belonging, the card players rate low in status. Their daily, continuous playing in the lounge is a constant provocation of criticism. Another change of policy was to regulate their hours of playing, to forbid it during the noon hour, and to insist, with considerable sharpness, that games cease whenever there is an announcement from the platform.

The community no longer tolerates quarrelsome or disruptive behavior, and when contentious card players become noisy they are promptly quelled by one of the officers, backed by the approval of the members. Here again the staff was slow in comprehending the extent to which group responsibility had advanced, or how much the individual had come to understand and accept the control of the group over his behavior, as the following incident will illustrate.

Mr. Finegold, aged 79, limited his activities to playing cards or chatting with only a few individuals, yet showed his need of the center by demanding, during a membership meeting, that it also be open in the evenings. When the president answered that this was a policy matter for the Board of Directors to decide he retorted on the contrary, that he, as president, was there to transmit the wishes of the membership to the Directors and to see that they were carried out. His suggestion was then tactfully made into a motion to be transmitted to the Board, and the administrative difficulties of opening the center evenings were discussed with him privately.

But his irascible temperament led him into frequent brawls, after which explosions he would stay away for days. Once, however, he kicked another member during one of these rows and there was a wave of indignation in the lounge. It happened that the Executive Committee was then in session upstairs, and the matter was reported to them. One of its officers appeared in the lounge and beckoned Mr. Finegold to follow him. With the lounge watching he went reluctantly. Once there he was offered a seat and solicitously asked if he had his heart pills with him. When he nodded the speaker advised him to take one. The behavior episode was then described and he was asked how he could justify it. He said defiantly that he was quick-tempered, and could not tolerate opposition because he was of the line of Levites, i.e., one of the elect. The worker who was present asked, if this episode had occurred in the street and a policeman had seen it, did he think that justification would have been accepted, and moreover, did not being a Levite imply the obligation of setting an example. Others spoke, and he was so chastened by this confrontation with the center's officers that he apologized to the committee. Yet far from being antagonized he seemed relieved by this procedure, resumed his game, and did not absent himself next day. This evidence of group control also satisfied the lounge, where there were no further comments on the episode.

The fact that the membership accepts the Executive Committee's role is also an end-product of group experience. Its sessions are the scenes of frequent and heated debate over center problems. But the conclusions reached by these discussions are then brought to the members, the reasons for them are presented, and the membership is asked to vote on the matter. Their feeling that this committee represents them is, therefore, firmly grounded on having shared in its decisions.

This progress in group performance is also demonstrated by the many program suggestions which have been made by the members and carried out. The barber shop service is one such, and we have already described how the then president took steps to cut short the delays in establishing it.

The need for a cafeteria was first pointed out by the members, and though its equipping and first servicing was done by the women's auxiliary, the main part of the menu planning, the cooking and the servicing has again been taken over by the members.

A recent suggestion to establish a shirt hospital was tried out and is doing well. This kind of service at cost has more than only practical values. Many who are able to turn collars and cuffs are glad to realize that their skill makes them needed and useful to others.

Some years ago, Mr. Mannheim, who had been a shoe-maker, suggested that we start a shoe repairing service. Such a service existed in one of the settlement houses of the city. A committee was organized to visit this agency and to make a full report. The facts and figures which they presented were favorable, but the committee, discussing it in member-ship meeting, agreed that lack of space for the necessary large machinery made the project impossible at present. However, this idea is merely waiting until more room is available to the community.

For the officers, as well as the membership, the institution of self-government has proved one of the most effective means of stimulating these older people to make use of their capacities. It has developed leadership, initiative, responsibility. It has served to focus attention and increase identification with the affairs of this community in even the least participating members.

CHAPTER FOUR

Programming

One of the difficulties of reporting the development of a group and the growth of an institution is that it must break into consecutive accounts phenomena which constitute a functional whole. In telling of the sequence of personalities who became officers of the club and how they and the members developed self-government, we carry the reader forward to the present, and give the current status as it evolved within the framework of that area of performance. But the center today is obviously the result of many activities, influences, and developments other than self-government, all of which were in constant interaction.

We can only hope to capture as many of these interacting elements as we were able to observe (how many may we not have overlooked!) by turning back repeatedly to the beginnings to single out another area of group experience, to see how individual attitudes have changed, the group changed, and the interaction between fellow members and with the workers developed.

Therefore, we now turn to programming, to review under this title the emergence of the diversified interests and special activities which played a role in transforming these unrelated individuals into a cohesive community.

Today when recreation facilities for the aged are no longer a novelty the various features of this program will be found to differ little from those set up everywhere throughout the country. For the same age groups they will vary only in accordance with the educational and economic backgrounds of the participants. We are therefore describing some of the separate items, not because any one activity in itself was unusual but because the stages of response to even the most familiar activities—cooking, serving, committees, parties—were stages symptomatic of growth in these old people. We repeat that the first objective for this particular group was to find ways of drawing them together, and any new activity was another means of giving them satisfactions, a sense of achievement, and the status which comes from winning the recognition and approval of their fellow-men. Because they are cut off from family and community contacts, old people are deprived of these basic needs, for even those who could read or knit found these occupations unrewarding if they could never discuss what they read or had no one for whom to knit. Therefore the first worker was led from one program item to the next by the members themselves as she watched for indications of interest or capacity to use in creating satisfactions and relationships. It was for this reason that group discussions of all plans were valuable. It was reassuring to an individual to venture a suggestion and have it acted upon. This might be his first step toward the group and their acceptance of his idea would start the cycle of interaction between him and them.

The women members illustrate this point. Although four of that early group were married and came to the center with their husbands, nevertheless at meetings they huddled with the other women at the rear of the room. The first woman to speak in meeting was admired by them for her boldness in creating a precedent. Shortly after this it was she who found a new way of preparing the coffee, by making bags which facilitated the preparation and the subsequent cleaning. After these two steps of independent activity she plunged into a third and far more important one, namely, to write an article for the newly organized center paper.

Its title "Proud as a Peacock" reflected a profound change

in her attitude toward the fact that she and her husband were receiving public assistance. Both had been employed all their lives, had been thrifty and hard working. Therefore, when they lost all their savings in an unfortunate investment, she felt a failure and was ashamed that they had to "depend on charity." The worker had discussed this feeling with her and presented a new point of view, namely, that their work had created wealth for the community and since they could no longer be active they had a right to this return for their past labors.

This new conception helped to dissipate her shame and her affirmation of it in the article again earned her status for another achievement.

We cite her case because these three steps happen to be so clear an example of successive activities which lead rapidly to a new release and adjustment in this community. It likewise illustrates the interaction between her efforts, the community's response, and the staff's role in enabling her to overcome feelings which were blocking her participation with the group. We were to watch for this pattern, and be alert to recognize the smallest signs of a new activity, knowing from experience that these were the moments of nascent change. When an uncommunicative sitter in the lounge once spontaneously emptied some ash trays the worker took that moment to ask him to show a newcomer around the center. She explained that she was too busy to do so herself and moreover, had not the advantage of speaking the stranger's language as he did. Confronted with the many characteristics common to old people—intolerance of others, envy, suspiciousness, fear of competition, timidity, and general insecurity—we assumed that they were not constitutional personality traits, but might be the results of cumulative and prolonged frustrations, and that they could be altered by offering new opportunities for satisfaction and personalized help in adjustment. Again and again we were to find this assumption justified and to observe that changes in attitude occurred continually and sometimes to see the reasons why they occurred just then.

We were also to see that the staff must be constantly alert to give the support these clients needed before they could again begin to try out their capacities. Many had so long resigned themselves to being shoved aside that when asked to do things and take responsibility they shrank back. It would take many satisfying experiences in this new milieu before their all-pervading insecurity was replaced by renewed confidence. For that reason it was so important to watch over each step, and to protect them from a sense of failure. When the first secretary became discouraged by his inadequate performance and wanted to resign, it was essential that he be made to see the small signs of his improvement and be helped to overcome his difficulties so that he finish out his term of office. Mr. Lowden's autocratic behavior as president might be far from representative government but it was still a form of leadership and as such must be cultivated. Therefore, the office of registrar was created to continue to give him status. As other signs of leadership appeared, further offices were created. Later, when crafts had been introduced and a bazaar was planned to give purpose to the things they were making, there were many too imperfect to put on sale. But all of them could be sold in grab bags.

Programming was not only gathering up into planned activities the indications of what they could and might like to do, but working from the level at which they did them, watchful to support each stage. When a center publication was introduced we published everything submitted. We edited only where the contribution might make the writer appear to disadvantage, and first discussed with him whether the change in wording more nearly expressed his meaning. How much these people needed success and recognition was evident when a contributor's name was once inadvertently omitted in publication. We apologized to the author and to membership for the error but before distribution she gathered up the edition to write her name into each of the 500 copies.

CHAPTER FIVE

Woodwork and Painting

In the following chapter we give in some detail the history of two of the first handicrafts because their introduction and the subsequent course of these projects were, in the field of crafts, the counterpart of the slow stirring into activity and new interest which took place in the total membership in those early days. There was a reason for this slow tempo of change.

During the war years when the center was opened, the man-power shortage enabled the more adequate older person to prolong his earning years. This group, gathered mainly from the lists of those receiving Old Age Assistance, were those either physically handicapped or otherwise not able to profit from this exceptional demand for workers. They were the ones who had been most damaged by prolonged isolation and idleness.

But there are additional reasons for reporting on these first crafts. Many visitors to the center, who come because they are in the first stages of organizing clubs for older people, ask us how to stimulate interest. They report with discouragement that old people are slow to take part, or else that those who do sample a new activity, often do not continue. These comments suggest a brief discussion in regard to all occupations and activities in this age group.

Both in the literature which deals with the problems of the aged and to the layman, the idea of introducing older people to arts and crafts, employing their leisure by inducing them to make things, finds ready acceptance. Indeed in recent years there has been a spate of articles recommending hobbies as the best preparation for retirement and implying that the pursuit of a hobby will serve to arm the older person against all the problems of adjustment in his later years.

While hobbies is a wide term which justifiably should include an unlimited repertoire of sustained interests, there are indications (in hobby shows, for instance) that it is frequently used as a synonym for arts and crafts. We wish to make use of this interchange of terms in order to examine the ideas associated with hobbies in general, as well as with arts and crafts in particular.

There is one purpose common to the most unusual of hobbies and the simplest of craft skills, namely, finding an interest with which to fill leisure time. Whether the retired individual engages in abstruse research or learns to hammer an ash tray, he is substituting this activity for the work which formerly filled his days. But his former job meant more than the fact that it occupied his time and earned his living. If he was fortunate it was also the expression of his main interest and of his individual capacities. But even if it was less fulfilling than this, it gave him a sense of his own worth. It brought him into contact with others and gave him his status and role, both economic and social. It gave routine and meaning to his days and the feeling of sustained and perhaps progressive adequacy.

Therefore retirement means far more than leisure from labor. It means finding substitutes for all that the job meant, other ways of continuing to feel that through usefulness and a purpose one still has status in the community. These social needs are suddenly left frustrated. Therefore whatever activity, hobby or craft is brought to the older person must supply more than mere occupation. In some measure it must satisfy these wider social needs as well.

We stress this point because in recording our experiences

with occupations for the older person we found that it was rarely the particular activity which was important in motivating an individual to take part. Instead, and especially in the first years, it was the social aspect which formed the strongest motivation, the drive to do what others were doing, or the desire to please the leader or to win approval from the group. In this respect the motives for trying new crafts were the same as those which impelled the older person to serve on committees, join the dramatics, music or poetry groups, or to run for office. In terms of social adjustment, arts and crafts are perhaps less rewarding activities than joining other groups or committees, for it is the interaction within the group which fosters responsiveness and flexibility and thus continues growth and adaptation.

Once we understand that all the occupations as well as the purely recreational activities which we offer the older person are resources with which he may fashion as satisfying a life as he can achieve, we will anticipate some of the reactions to each item of our program repertoire. We will see with a more discerning eye what is taking place and realize, as some of the following records show, that a lonely and maladjusted individual may seem objectively to be accomplishing little in the craft group he has joined, yet show beneficial results in his general behavior and in his changing attitudes towards this new opportunity of being with people.

We have seen how the whole group responded to leadership and joint planning for the club. We would now describe the course of an occupation which was started shortly after these beginnings. If we give in somewhat pedestrian detail the steps of this project, it is because observing them will help us to realize that whatever our clients undertake, each will do it in his own way, for his own reasons, and therefore, the results must be measured in terms of our understanding of that individual's total needs rather than by his specific craft skill.

But we would stress again that the individual's basic needs are social as well as personal. The two crafts which we have selected to report reflected the interaction of social adjustments and personal needs as they were fostered and satisfied by these activities. We chose them solely because they happened to have been introduced to the program early in the center's history. Nor do we believe that it was the particular activity which was responsible for the growth and changes which the record shows, but that the same process would have taken place within the framework of any other activity.

Woodworking was one of the first handicrafts introduced at the center. There were practical reasons for selecting this occupation. The center was on a limited budget, it was war time, and this material could be obtained by donations of waste lumber. Moreover, the worker was casting about for a craft to interest the men. Except for the few who took to painting (of which we shall report presently) the rest so far had been spending their time playing games, and she was eager to provide them with a greater variety of interests. She had made some efforts to stimulate those who had previous experience to continue woodworking at the center, but they responded only when there was some specific assignment such as shelves which were needed for the club.

She therefore engaged a teacher of carpentry and when he arrived, told the members that a class in woodwork would be formed. She spoke of the kind of things which could be made: articles for themselves or their homes, toys for their grandchildren, things for the center, or articles which could be sold at a bazaar. She spoke of the mental and physical benefits of such work; the revival of old skills and the development of new. Under the stimulus of this talk sixteen enrolled for the class.

Only eight appeared when the work was to begin. The shop was set up in the basement, reached by a narrow flight of stairs. This was an obstacle.

Only one of the group had any definite plans in mind. Mr. Goodman said he wanted to make a night table. The teacher therefore suggested that they all work on this together. They did so reluctantly and the following week only four came to the session. When the poor attendance was discussed, the members said they objected to working in the basement and to making a table for Mr. Goodman. Mr. Blackman, who had brought his own tools and felt he needed no instruction, now moved them upstairs and sitting in a corner busied himself with the construction of a doll's house.

After several weeks it became clear that some other means of stimulation must be found or the class would cease. The teacher therefore made use of the birthday party to demonstrate the assembly of various simple articles for which he had pre-cut the parts. At the same time one of the Department of Welfare Staff who was present gave a talk on the values of craft activities.

It was decided to move the class upstairs to the lounge. The worker had obtained cut-outs of animals to be assembled into toys and suggested that they be made to give to some nursery school. There was renewed interest and several men volunteered to help in moving the tools and materials upstairs and setting up a workshop in an area adjoining the lounge.

Thirteen men joined this new class, and the work was divided into separate processes: sawing, nailing, drilling, sandpapering, and painting. Only two of this group had had any previous experience in working with wood. Five had done manual work, such as electrician's helper, polisher, painter or weaver. The others had been clerks, salesmen, or furriers. Those with the greatest manual dexterity chose the sawing, gluing, and nailing processes; those with the least, did the sandpapering. In this new location, visible to the rest of the club, the group worked together once a week until all the toys had been assembled. A few even worked between sessions when the teacher was not there.

The project fostered considerable interaction among its participants. They began telling each other about their previous work experiences, and while working together grew to know each other better and to become friendly.

When the toys were finished the worker made much of the plan to give them to a nursery school. The one selected was in a nearby settlement house known to some of the club. Members other than the woodworkers helped to pack the toys. A committee of two was elected to take them to the school. At the next membership meeting this committee reported on the presentation and read aloud the letter of thanks from the settlement house. By these devices she managed to endow the project with as much importance as possible and to enable the entire membership to feel that they also shared in its community effects.

She later used the same means to solve the problem of toys which had not been sold at the bazaar. Again they were donated to nursery schools, presented by two committee members who reported on the presentation and read the letters of thanks to the membership.

The most effective results of this procedure came when some eyeglass cases, which had not appealed to the bazaar shoppers, were sent to the sight conservation class of a public school. The worker knew the teacher of this class and the latter then reciprocated the gift by having the children make book markers to be used in the club library.

It is never possible to say just what are the benefits of such steps, nor to claim that they establish community relations. But this was in the first year of the center, when most of these old people were only beginning to feel at home in the club, and while most of them were still burdened with a sense of their uselessness. The project gave them a conception of still being able to be of service to others, and what was especially appealing, to be of service to children who reciprocated their gifts. The disappointment of having made unsalable articles was thus counteracted and those who had made them, as well as the whole group, had satisfaction and pride in this accomplishment.

But interest again waned as summer came and the teacher was on vacation. Mr. Blackman, who had not helped in the toymaking, continued to work on his doll house. Two of the group also began to build miniature houses and to make doll's furniture.

By the time the teacher returned in autumn, the worker had often spoken of holding a bazaar and the men now suggested making articles of wood for sale. The teacher brought gouging tools whose use was new to the group, and presently an electric lathe, drill and jigsaw were added to the equipment. With the stimulus of learning to use the new tools, a constantly expanding variety of objects to make, and the interest and approval of the whole membership, who watched the work from the lounge, this activity now gained considerable momentum.

Since woodworking was one of the first projects and involved men whom it was hard to interest in anything, we would like to summarize some of the individual records on this activity. They show a variety of changes in behavior as this work went on, and some of the individual needs which were met by this occupation.

Mr. Heim, aged 62, a former ironworker and cantor, had been at the center almost a year. He lived in a furnished room, had neither friends nor family, and had constant difficulty in getting along with people. He had a severe cardiac condition, and was deaf. At the center he sang, not occasionally, but constantly, and at all times, and was oblivious to the resentment this aroused. He had a continual feud with his Department of Welfare investigator, and at first was suspicious of the worker because of her connection with that agency. Nevertheless he began to visit the craft shop to please her and finally decided she was his friend.

At the class he talked about the things he was going to make but was always postponing the work, puttering around, helping others by holding boards or making trimmings for their projects. His span of attention was short. He never worked more than half an hour, during which he perspired copiously. But while in the shop he was less tense, expressed less hostility toward others, and as a result their resentment and scornful attitude toward him changed. He had been conspicuously unkempt and now began to make efforts to improve his appearance. He became friendlier toward the worker and showed it by no longer singing whenever he pleased. Instead, he accepted her suggestion to sing only when invited to do so at parties.

Here the activity was of minimal importance, but the associations it offered were able to make some headway against his pattern of tension, reactive hostility, and expectation of rejection.

Mr. Solen, aged 69, was a former caner who had never worked with wood but who had considerable manual dexterity. He needed much persuasion to join the group and though he was interested in watching others, worked only when there was a specific job to be done for the center or a member, such as repairing furniture or making some article of use for someone. He got on with others and this association was more important to him than the work. His help in repairing center furniture gave him a feeling of belonging and won him both respect and admiration from the members. He too had a cardiac condition and worked for only one hour at a time, with frequent rests, but he was flexible toward his ailment and varied his rest periods according to how he felt.

Mr. Rieser, aged 74, was a former cabinet maker who enjoyed working with wood, but preferred to do so at home rather than in the class. However, he brought the things he had made at home to show the class and his skill in carving and creating novel cigarette boxes, or in making things needed at the center, such as easels, gave him a special status which he valued. He rarely worked in the group except to help others.

Six men, ranging in age from 64 to 81, limited their activity to the toy project and all but one to the process of sandpapering. None had had any previous experience and needed much encouragement to begin. They chose this process as the least skilled, two of them because of poor eyesight, the other four because they were insecure and preferred the job at which they could be sure of not failing. All began talking and joking with each other and the two who were most withdrawn, one a Negro and the other a Pole who spoke no English, seemed more relaxed and managed to communicate with the others in the group.

In all these cases the social aspects of the activity were more important than what they were doing. They overcame physical handicaps, lack of interest, or fear of failure for the sake of doing something with others and being in the swim. But once these reluctant men had made the first step other effects followed. There was more branching out into individual projects. Mr. S. and Mr. B. began to build a miniature Hebrew altar, and while helping them to complete it Mr. P., a Catholic, showed much interest in the rituals of the synagogue as the others explained the meaning and uses of the altar.

Mr. Kramer, aged 68, came to the center in the autumn of 1945, when all the activity revolved around the coming bazaar. Although a quiet, withdrawn person, he needed little urging to join the woodworkers since he already had some skill in this field. He had once been an iron worker and more recently had sold dry goods, but had always enjoyed making things for his home. Therefore this project gave him an immediate opportunity to do work he liked and at which he felt competent while getting to know others. He worked independently and finished a napkin holder which was praised by the teacher and the members. This encouraged him to continue to make other things for the bazaar: match box holders, corner shelves, etc. He was eager to learn how to make new objects, accepted guidance from the teacher, and mastered the use of the jigsaw, although with some timidity—using it only when the instructor was nearby. He was careful in using tools and materials and very orderly. His cardiac condition limited his periods of working but he worked two hours at a time with rests at half-hour intervals. As he grew friendly with others, although he worked independently, he helped them and sought their help. He was proud of the fact that they admired his work and that even the retired carpenters found it hard to believe that this was merely a hobby and not his means of livelihood.

His wife came to see him work and urged him to make furniture for their home. She was glad that he had found a place to pursue his hobby where she did not have to clean up after him. As he continued to work he seemed less tense and noticeably more at ease and friendly with the members. He began to come to the meetings and to the parties.

To this member the work itself was of first importance. He still had a home and the companionship of his wife as well as affectionate relations with his married daughter. Yet finding a new setting in which to do the work he enjoyed gradually brought a change in his attitude, until in addition to the work, he also wanted to share in the club's other activities and social gatherings. Because the center and its staff began to mean more to him, he presently followed the worker's suggestion that he also try painting. He was skeptical toward the idea at first but nevertheless became interested and was quick to learn. The fortunate timing of this second hobby was to serve him well, for not long after his first successful experiments in painting he had a heart attack which made it impossible for him to continue the work which had meant so much to him.

Today the center has a large and well equipped workshop

in charge of an occupational therapist, and woodwork is only one of the many crafts in operation there.

Yet even within this one craft alone we can observe the same differences in competence of the present woodworkers compared with that group nine years ago, which is reflected throughout the rest of the center membership. Though there are also those who try to do woodwork as a new interest, many of the others who do carpentry or cabinet making have come to the center soon after retirement. Their confidence and ability have not been impaired. They are already skilled in woodwork and come to the shop because they are glad to find the tools and space to do the work they like. Some make ambitious projects such as chairs and benches for their own use. Others, equally skilled, find great satisfaction in designing and making much needed cabinets and storage closets for the shop itself or for other center rooms. Their skillful workmanship and the great usefulness of their products give them status, not only in the shop but in the center at large.

A social adjustment and group formation has taken place within the shop area throughout the years that it has been in operation. When it was first made available we noticed that it was the more withdrawn older person who went to the shop, as though he depended on his craft skill for satisfactions which did not, or could not, include social relationships.

Mr. Blackman is an extreme example of this point. In the first year of the center this introverted, crochety individual, short and hunchbacked, was only interested in carpentry. He built himself a kind of cage in a corner of the room, and worked within this area, each evening carefully snapping the padlock which he had put on the door. The attendance at this time was still small enough and the members all still so diffident and insecure that the worker's policy was a permissiveness both unnecessary and impossible today. Yet it was interesting to watch the slight changes in Mr. Blackman's behavior, to see him gradually begin to leave the door open, and finally to work outside his cage, using it only to store his tools at the end of the day.

The shop has added many crafts to its repertoire, work with metal, plastics, weaving, jewelry making, carving, rush work, ceramics, painting. For a considerable time, however, those who worked there did so as a parallel activity, each at his own skill, rather than as a cooperative effort such as had been contrived during the time of the toy project.

But gradually several factors served to weld the shop workers into a self-conscious group. The focal point of this group formation was furnished by the occupational therapist to whom they could attach themselves. She made use of this relationship to stimulate their interest and attention to each other's work. She discussed general shop problems with them at special shop meetings, conducted by the same democratic methods as membership meetings. She also contrived ways of extending their interest to matters which concerned the whole center. All of these devices served to increase their group awareness and to bind them together.

At first they used to join the others in the lounge at noon, but presently they began bringing their refreshments to the shop. They arranged to have an electric heater for their coffee and delegated their own committee to do the serving. The women made table mats of oilcloth, work was stopped, and the noon hour has become a leisurely and festive period.

Formerly, while it was still possible to seat everyone in the lounge during birthday parties, the shop group asked to have a reserved table at which they could sit together. Today when the attendance at parties is too large to seat all in that area, the shop workers do not feel this is an exclusion, but decorate their work tables and indeed are mildly reluctant to have an extra table there used to accommodate the overflow from the lounge. The shop has become a center within the center, and those who find their first satisfying experiences there, branch out from that home base to try other activities.

If in this report of one craft we seem to have minimized the benefits to an individual which stem directly from craft skill—the satisfactions of manual dexterity, the pleasures of creative effort—it is not because we undervalue them. When and where they occur, they are easy to observe and one is not likely to overlook them. But in an age group where craft skills, especially those newly learned, are acquired slowly and the results are often less than perfect, it is the needs of the total personality which we want to stress, and to share our observations of the ways in which benefits from a group setting for handicrafts showed themselves in various individuals.

We would like to add one more individual record from this area of activity which has to do with the selection of a craft. However varied our repertoire, the needs of the individual are still more various and to find an occupation which is satisfying is in itself a creative search and achievement.

The multicraft shop offers much stimulus to watching and to experimenting with various media.

Mr. Eberfeld is an illustration of the course of such experimenting. He is a refugee from Germany where he had gone through shattering experiences. Five of his children were killed by the Nazis and he and his wife spent years in a concentration camp. His wife is older than he, and an invalid. When he first came to the center he still showed the effects of his experiences. He seemed timid and constrained and his hands trembled. In Europe he had been a free lance journalist, writing in French, German and Yiddish, but was not fluent in English. This work, however, would no longer have been possible even in a foreign language newspaper since he has hardening of the arteries, and is frequently blocked in finding words, acutely aware of this difficulty, and dissatisfied with anything he now writes.

One worker made her contact with him in German and when he said he would like to learn to use a typewriter, arranged to lend him one. He seemed very touched when she suggested that he take it home so that he could be with his wife while practicing. It was during this talk that he showed her the tattooed number on his arm and also the armband with the yellow star which he had been forced to wear in the concentration camp.

He was very doubtful that he could do woodwork since he had never used his hands, but agreed that doing manual work might counteract the thoughts which haunted him. He made a small plant shelf for his wife and was pleased with this accomplishment, though rather lukewarm about working with wood.

Later he tried copper repoussé work and decided to make a wall plaque. This was his first creative work with his hands and it was deeply moving to see what he had made. It was the Star of David, intricately and beautifully designed, converting into an adornment for his home the emblem of his terrible experience.

He is a gentle and sensitive person, very responsive to what he felt to be the interest and good will of the staff. In the small community of the shop he slowly began to make friends. But, though he explored every available medium in the shop, pounding heavy copper into ash trays, and experimenting with leather work, he still seemed dissatisfied with these occupations.

Presently when a new painting teacher came he suggested with some hesitation that he would like to try this. He made fun of his first efforts, commenting that old people were childish to do such things. Yet painting absorbed him more and more, and he has continued it for many months with steadily improving skill.

The worker wondered whether he had not had resistance to the other crafts because they all seemed childish pastimes to him in contrast to his former work as journalist and free lance writer. She knew how his recurrent aphasic symptoms distressed him for he had spoken of the moments when he could not find words or "can't seem to think at all." She therefore commented one day that while formerly he used words to make pictures and to communicate, now he was doing so with paint. He seemed to appreciate this concept, for he agreed with a quick lightening of expression.

This was only a guess at the meaning and value of painting to Mr. Eberfeld. It expressed the worker's hope that an indication of understanding his problem might give him support in whatever he was seeking in this experience.

He was concentrated when at work, with a visible relaxation of expression and posture. Recently his frail and ailing wife was taken to the hospital for what may be a fatal operation. He visits her daily and is shaken by this new threat to their reconstructed life. Yet he still comes daily to paint for a few hours, explaining that it fortifies him for these visits and for the hours when he is alone in their apartment.

Painting, which was started as early as carpentry, was far more of an experimental venture to this group. Yet 14 of the 40 members made a beginning, although only two of this group had ever painted before. Nor had they the benefit of prolonged instruction, for at that time it was possible to secure a teacher for only two sessions—as a courtesy loan from a nearby settlement house. It was therefore all the more striking that this interest should have taken hold as it did, and continued through the lean years when instruction was not available to blossom again when a stimulating teacher could be secured.

Here too we began noting the social factors which influenced this highly individual occupation. For just as Mr. Blackman, as an extreme example of introversion, gradually came out of his cage to do his carpentering, so those who began to paint responded to this activity in varying proportions of interest in painting itself, and in the people with whom they painted.

Despite the support of a teacher, that initial group was so timid at that first session that the staff worker said she too had never painted and was eager to try with them. This seemed to help them to start.

The one member who had asked to have painting lessons added to the program was prevented by illness from attending these classes and was deeply disappointed at losing this opportunity. This was Mr. Schultz, already known to us as the first vice-president, and who was to add this interest to his many other activities and to achieve considerable success in this field.

When the teacher left, five of the fourteen dropped out. Only two of this class had ever painted before; one, Mr. Bank, had begun at 40; the other, Mr. Sullivan, had taught himself from the age of 64. Though he has continued to paint throughout the years he has done so at home, but in the absence of a teacher was helpful to others in instructing them how to prepare a canvas and to sketch in a composition. It was he who started Mr. Schultz, whose background as house-painter made him familiar with the mixing of color. Both of these men preferred to work at home rather than in a class, but when a teacher was again secured, Mr. Schultz brought his canvasses for criticism and approval. He painted land-scapes, some from nature, but also imaginary scenes such as "The Village Street on Christmas Eve." The style was primitive and they had great liveliness and charm. They were much admired at subsequent bazaars and many were sold, so that he had the pleasure and encouragement of praise and unexpected earnings.

As the class continued by themselves, there was considerable spread in the use of media. Mr. Sullivan and Mr. Schultz concentrated on oil painting; others preferred to draw, using both charcoal and pencil. Mrs. Mishkin, who had been mentioned earlier as preferring "intellectual activities" to helping with the serving committee, drew curious charcoal compositions of men or brides. She worked both at home and at the center, continuing for about six months. She made little progress in comparison with the others and probably for that reason stopped her attempts as the others improved.

But despite so little instruction in an art foreign to all but two, the group continued, and watching their efforts impelled newcomers to try.

Mr. Darb, for instance, remembered doing drawings in school at the age of twelve, but now knew neither the names of colors nor how to mix them. He began drawing in charcoal and as the leader showed him how to mix colors, learned quickly and eagerly. He went to the library and looked at art books, copying from them. The leader then suggested that he paint the things he saw about him at the center. He did a huge painting in oils of the lounge. The perspective was crude, but this reproduction of the club setting obviously gave him great pleasure and brought him much praise from the other members. It was framed and hung in the lounge. The worker then encouraged him to join an art class in a nearby settlement where he could have instruction. He showed considerable tension at first until the teacher began praising his work.

Mr. Darb's themes have continued to be settings which mean much to him: a Seder scene, and recently a painting of his room. This is considerably idealized as to spaciousness, but done with a quality of loving detail as though in painting he had found a creative magic by which to make the homely things of his surroundings reflect inner feelings which give him support. This particular painting is especially significant because it was done at the end of a long absence from the center, when his arthritis had so crippled him that he could no longer come. His social contacts meant much to him and he was well liked. Yet he sent word that he wished no visitors and finally confided to a friend who met him on the street that it was because he was unable to keep his room tidy or clean and therefore was ashamed to have visitors. After two years absence he was so much better that he could return, as immaculately groomed as formerly, and brought this painting in which he had transformed the dinginess of his room in which his illness had imprisoned him.

Others also revealed personal attitudes either in their paintings or in their valuation of them.

Mr. Meinhut, aged 72, is a rigid, insecure person, quick in all his movements, with rapid speech often accompanied by a short laugh, which does not change the sharp, hostile expression of his eyes. He had been a wood carver and the worker therefore suggested that he might be interested in the art class. He began by drawing designs of flowers such as might be used in carving. Since he seemed unwilling to use paints, he was given watercolor pencils which pleased him.

He copied pictures from newspapers, magazines and books. His drawings steadily improved with practice, but he used the pencils faintly as though the bold use of color were beyond the rigid confines of his personality. His pictures were either copies of famous Jewish leaders, or pious Jews in prayer; or he created startlingly grotesque cartoons, reminiscent of the Police Gazette in which someone suffers a ludicrous mishap.

He was unable to accept criticism from anyone or to grant approval to the work of others. If he agreed that he liked a painting done by someone else, he would express doubt that the member had actually done it himself. He constantly set a price on his own creations, never under $100, though none was ever sold. Yet he worked long stretches, whole afternoons, and was enormously gratified by any approving comment of his efforts. A few were framed and hung in the lounge and he was incensed when a half-opened door temporarily hid one of his cartoons. He made a few superficial relationships to others at the center. His one activity was drawing, which he gradually began to do at home as much as at the club. Yet such satisfaction and social relationships as he was able to attain came through or in connection with this interest.

Through the years there have been other times when a teacher has again been secured. One was a young artist of considerable talent with a warm and outgoing personality, and under his guidance new members joined the classes. He did many charcoal sketches of the members, and being selected as a model was a flattering attention. He also arranged to take a group to an art museum and this was a startling experience to some. One man said, "Forty years I have lived and worked in this city and never knew that there were places just to show pictures." He also took them to the park to sketch. These various outings, his own sincere and eager interest in each individual's work and style, his encouragement, discussions, and support of their efforts, all greatly increased the group feeling and what had been a parallel activity now created relationships between the participants. Mr. Darb was especially attached to this artist and during this time devoted most of his energy to painting. He was delighted to be selected by the teacher to pose as his model in his classes at an art museum, a role both gratifying and remunerative.

This artist had skill and tact in teaching so that the members made progress during his sessions. Mr. Schultz, who so far had had no professional instruction, brought his specific problems, and though he still preferred to work at home applied the solutions with obvious profit.

Two other members may be cited to illustrate the effects which painting had on their total adjustment. Neither had had any experience in drawing since childhood, and at first each was astonished and amused at the suggestion that they paint, yet both in time made this their major activity at the center and at home.

Mr. Schafter, aged 70, a refugee from Austria, had been coming to the center for two years. He is a man of superior education, a former bank teller, but though he had been in the United States for six years, spoke little English. He attended the English classes and was able to read and write fairly well but was unable to understand spoken English. He seemed to have a certain pride in this handicap and would discuss his difficulty in German with considerable elaboration. Two things were obvious in such discussions: his feeling of his own cultural superiority to the other members, and his tense and timid personality which made it hard for him to interest himself in any one.

He had had a desolating experience in Austria during the

war when he lost contact with his only child, a daughter from whom he has never heard since. This constant worry colored all his thoughts though he was afraid to take steps to learn the facts. When the English classes terminated for the summer the worker felt it was necessary to give him an affiliation with another small group and suggested that he join the art class. He agreed partly to please her and partly out of curiosity and discovered that he had real talent.

At first he needed to have the teacher's instructions translated but as his skill and satisfaction increased so did his ability to understand English. At first he constantly sought reassurance by showing his work and making derisive comments about it, saying he was exhibiting his "latest crime." He worked well from models and practised again and again to achieve "perfection." He began to work at home, doing sketches of his wife and neighbors, and presently was saying that he liked some of his paintings. He did a mural which was framed, then hung in the lounge and unveiled at a membership meeting. On this occasion he so far conquered his resistances as to be able to make an English speech of thanks to the members for their applause, but assured them that he was not an artist.

While he has not made friends whom he sees outside the center, his relationships there have noticeably improved. His tension has greatly decreased and his wife feels that his painting is a "Godsend"; at least he forgets himself for several hours a day. He continues the English classes, but his interest in them is subordinate to his interest in painting.

His best work is in portraiture. The only freely creative work which he has done was for a short period when he painted several compositions, aggressive in mood, with lowering skies, jagged by lightning, and a foreground of bombs and rockets exploding among all the symbols of modern civilization. These pictures and an occasional poem in German, deeply pessimistic in tone but ably composed, are the two outlets through which he now channelizes a trauma that formerly haunted his mind and which he can now externalize through creative efforts.

We have mentioned Mr. Kramer previously in discussing woodwork. The staff noticed that he liked to paint designs on his wooden articles and suggested that he join the art class.

He was amused and laughed heartily at the idea, but one afternoon when it was too hot to use the power saws he came to the class. His first attempts were very crude but he enjoyed the session and returned to it the following week. He showed definite progress and soon began creating interesting compositions using chalk pastels.

He had had few educational opportunities and this was a new experience. He responded well to instruction and revealed a sensitive discrimination of color and detail. He did imaginative landscapes and once a woman praying over candles. He too had never seen an art museum and was so delighted when the group visited one that he remained after the others had left and planned to return with his wife.

Several months later he had a heart attack which later prevented his continuing work with wood and heavy machinery. But it did not interfere with his painting. His wife reported that this helped him through the convalescence since he could not be idle. His daughter was impressed with his work and many of his paintings hang in her home. Whenever his health permits he comes to the center to paint, and does charming snow scenes for Christmas cards which sell well. Here too a new activity served its participant during a period of readjustment.

It would seem that painting is one of the least social activities, yet in reviewing the painting at the center the interaction of the participants was a constant and important factor. True that two of the best painters preferred to work at home, but the approval and criticism of the group was a factor in their motivation. So was the lack of improvement compared with others which made Mrs. Mishkin drop out. The last two cases cited, who have continued throughout the years, are both married and it may be that having companionship at home makes it less necessary that painting satisfy their social needs and that in their cases it is more truly an interest in the activity itself. And finally, we would note also the kind of self-expression which painting also serves. Mr. Meinhut's aggressions found an outlet in his cartoons; Mr. Schafter's preoccupying trauma was pictured in scenes of destruction; and Mr. Darb, imprisoned by illness in his room, was able to transform its disorder into a setting which reflected his standards and desires.

CHAPTER SIX

Poetry

The history of the poetry reading group was another area of activity which showed patterns of individual change and new development, and of the interactions between the group and the individual.

This was the first group to be formed around an interest rather than a craft, and the activity suggested itself to the worker as a way of combining the special talent of one member with a closer relationship to others.

Mr. Sullivan was a tense, somewhat rigid and extremely reserved man who came to the center daily but remained aloof from the others and spent most of his time reading or listening to the radio. The worker gradually learned that he was born in Ireland of Protestant parents, that he was married and had one daughter, but she also inferred that he never mentioned the center to them.

One day he showed her some verses he had written about the club and said he had been writing verses for several years and had formerly belonged to a poetry writers' group in the borough. He was greatly pleased when she suggested that others at the center might like to meet weekly to hear his poems and to read poetry to each other. It came about quite naturally that he took the lead in the first such poetry meeting by reading one of his own.

As the group grew and the center's space was expanded, they moved to another room where the chairs are arranged in rows facing a desk. Mr. Sullivan then took the desk chair and for nine years has presided at these meetings. The worker sits near him, takes the attendance and has been careful not to intrude on his role of leader.

Mr. Sullivan's procedure is to give some brief introduction to his poem, either about its contents or the circumstances which prompted him to write it; then after reading it, he calls on each member in turn to read whatever he has selected. There is applause and comment, sometimes discussion about the poems, and generally there is time for a second round of reading.

Over the years there has been a marked improvement in the level of the selections. At first most of them were verses clipped from the local newspapers. But gradually, as the library was amplified by donated books, the staff introduced the group to anthologies and so helped them to become familiar with a wider range of poetry.

To many members reading aloud even simple prose is a difficult feat, either because they are foreign-born, or because, though Americans, their schooling has been limited. Yet week after week such difficult readers expose themselves to this challenge, often with intense nervousness and embarrassment, followed by obviously immense satisfaction of accomplishment.

Here lies at least one clue to the persisting devotion of the group to this activity. It is not primarily appreciation of poetry which holds their interest, but the fact that they are doing something together in which each one has a part, that the group will respond to each contribution, and that to all of them, foreign-born or native, the activity has a prestige value as being "educational." And finally, by the applause each contributor is stimulated anew to further cooperation. In no other activity is there quite so uncomplicated a pattern of performance and reaction to it, of mutual encouragement and appreciation of each other's efforts.

The records of successive staff observers also show an inter-

POETRY 87

esting similarity of pattern in each session. There is often
restlessness at the beginning, talking to each other, a comparing of selections, and other signs of nervous tension as
each one's turn approaches. Gradually the group's reaction to
each offering makes headway against this individual self-
absorption. There is routine applause for each performer,
but comments become more frequent, discussions spring up
stemming from the content of the poems. The group becomes relaxed and united in mood—either serious, gay, or
even hilarious where humorous poems happen to have pre-
dominated. Comments are of two kinds: those having to do
with performance, to which we will return later, and those
relating to content.

Those relating to content often lead to descriptions of past
experiences, expressions of opinion, of attitudes or statements
of life values, etc. These are opportunities for an individual
self-expression of a kind different from that in any other
group and conspicuous also in the choice of poems.

One would expect the range of selection to vary in accordance with the constituency of the group, i.e., with their educational and cultural backgrounds. But there are certain
clear trends both in the content of the selections and in the
applause and comment which they elicit. There is a pre-
dominance of poems which stress that not money or fame,
but kindness, the homely virtues, serenity and pleasure in
simple things, are the real values of life. Other choices also
tend to fall into categories, the poems familiar to them in
their youth, "The Boy Stood on the Burning Deck," etc., etc.,
or those which deal with youth, the country, changes of sea-
son, or the family and the home. Consolation for life's defeats, poems familiar from school days or those which evoke
memories of the sheltered happiness of youth have an appeal
that is not hard to understand.

Performance is not always confined to reading verses.
Sometimes people recite from memory, or read a prose selec-

tion, or even relate a story or joke. Such individual variations are part of the kind of self-expression these sessions
make possible. Mr. McCarthy, aged 80, twice recited a long
poem and this prodigious feat of memory was enthusiastically
applauded.

It may seem from this formalized pattern of procedure that
this activity never moves ahead, yet closer examination of the
records shows that there is a constant variation in the individual satisfaction and therefore, because this is a close-knit
group, also in that of the group-as-a-whole.

We have mentioned the encouragement of each other's
performance as a binding factor, but the group's self-feeling
is also strengthened by the inadequate performance of a poor
reader.

Mrs. Figler is a case in point. Her reading is barely in-
telligible. She herself certainly does not understand the selections she chooses at random, according to length, from the
anthologies available. Yet she persists, reading in a low voice,
hands shaking with nervousness, and finishes with a quick
little bob to the audience. She is rewarded with approving
comments on "her effort and her progress." It is perhaps true
that her very limitations, plus her persistence, afford them
group satisfaction.

If Mrs. Figler's elementary efforts reinforce the group's
feeling of superiority, another kind of response is called forth
by the following case:

Mr. Sobolski is blind and first came to the sessions as
listener. But presently he was impelled to bring selections
which he had typed in Braille so that he could also contribute. When his turn came the group listened in deep silence,
watching with fascination and pity as his fingers slid over
the raised dots of his paper. The applause was heartwarming
and tremendous.

He looks younger than most of the members and was admitted by special circumstances to this group. But the specta-

cle of his blindness, conquered by this strange skill of touch reading, stirred everyone, as though his efforts to participate in their chosen activity gave a moving confirmation of its value. Their warmth toward him in turn stimulated him to compose his own poems which signified to the group a new and special level of achievement for which they felt responsible. The fact that he is brought to the center once a week in order to be with this group, and that he recognizes many by their voices is another element in heightening their feeling of group closeness.

Sometimes this small group enables an individual to share an emotional experience of great meaning to himself in this new environment. Mr. Sidar is a Russian who through a long life in the needle trade in this country probably found no way of communicating the feelings and memories of his youth. He was introduced to this group because it seemed a way of bringing him into contact with others. After several sessions of listening he too explored the anthologies, and then rose one day to explain with real excitement that he had found a marvelous thing, a poem ". . . it tells just as I knew it in Russia when I was a boy about a man who shoes horses . . ."—and began reading "Under A Spreading Chestnut Tree."

In the past year there has been an increasing proportion of this group who have begun to write their own verses. It is probable that having a fellow-member, Mr. Sullivan, as leader, is responsible for this development, and that a staff worker would not have succeeded in giving them the confidence to make these attempts. Often these verses were mere jingles, first essays in the rhyming of words, but others reveal imagination and a high degree of poetic feeling. The following was written by a woman of 72, a Negro born in Haiti:

> Now that our feet are no longer
> Buoyant and swift
> Let us not murmur
> Because we are old and gray.
> Rather give God thanks
> For helping us through the many trials of life
> To become old.

The flowers bloom and then fade
When their petals fall.
They fall not in vain
But give their succor
To the other plants that take their places.

When we have ended life's journey
May we be like the petals—
Leaving some good deeds behind us
Which will help others on life's pathway.
Let us endeavor to do the best we can
Until we reach the last milestone.

CHAPTER SEVEN

Birthday Parties

From the beginning the center staff recognized the values of two kinds of groups—the small groups organized around a particular interest, and mass activities which would involve the whole membership. Today there are a variety of the latter: the monthly membership meeting, the celebration of holidays, outings, lectures and movies, and finally, one which also occurs monthly, the birthday party. While the rest of the list obviously appeals to diverse levels of interest, the birthday celebration has an importance all its own to this age group.

There are several reasons why this monthly gathering should stand out among all other mass activities. For most of the members this day of personal significance has lost whatever early associations of attention and celebration it may once have had. As one member put it, ". . . for 40 years I've been celebrating my children and grandchildren's birthdays . . . but I forget to celebrate my own." While he still has such family occasions to look forward to, most of the members are not so fortunate and indeed have almost forgotten the day of their birth. Some foreign-born members, especially Russian-born Jews, have no official records of their birth, nor can they identify on an American calendar this one day of the year as their own. And finally some come from families too large and too poor ever to have received this individual attention.

It is therefore a matter of surprise and sudden pleasure to find that one of the few questions asked on their arrival at the center is this date, together with the explanation that it will be celebrated here.

Even the birthday cards which are mailed have great meaning. One woman brought hers to show to a staff worker, then anxiously asked her to hand it back since it was the first mail she had received in fifteen years and she wanted to keep it in her handbag. It takes a constant effort of the imagination to realize the importance of such small attentions and to be sensitively aware of the human needs revealed by these responses, since staff workers have never experienced such privations.

We have already reported how the first birthday party was arranged for a member. Today, birthday celebrations seem to be a universal feature of old-age programs. But at the center that celebration also happened to be the first general party and the members' pleasure in such a new experience made them quick to mention the next individual whose day was approaching. As a result there were three such parties in one week. The worker suggested that their program planning should anticipate a growing membership and set aside one day a month for a joint celebration. It was also natural to combine with this event whatever national holidays fall within the month, using them as theme for the decorations, the musical program, or for talks.

More than any other mass activity this monthly event serves to intensify the community feeling. For the birthday-ites its appeal is personal, often deeply moving, as though they were overwhelmed to find themselves the center of attention, even though they share these honors with some sixty others at the birthday tables.

To the rest it promises one gala occasion a month to which to look forward on a calendar often devoid of such expectations. Clothing and grooming show the festive feeling. One woman's annual birthday present from her husband is a permanent wave, even though all the other days of the year her appearance is conspicuously unkempt.

The preparations for the party involve many otherwise non-participating individuals. The waiters' committee was carefully selected from the card players who rarely volunteer their services yet who were, each one, obviously pleased to be asked to help. A donation of white coats gives them conspicuous status. They meet before serving to discuss their stations, and the best procedure for maximum efficiency. They are served first and their contribution to everyone's comfort is mentioned with thanks from the platform. The work of making decorations, preparing the refreshments and serving, as well as the inevitable cleaning-up, are too easily taken for granted compared with the efforts of those who have a more conspicuous role on the entertainment program. The staff is therefore careful to see that these contributions receive their share of the applause.

Years ago the refreshment committee managed all the work of these parties. Today a special lunch is served and the women's auxiliary has taken over this large-scale job. Yet the original committee members still come to help on this day as though they felt a special responsibility toward this gala occasion.

The program of entertainment serves to give the singing and other music groups a community purpose in addition to their enjoyment of their weekly meetings.

It is also an excellent way of channelling the aggressive self-assertion of individuals. To make a speech, sing a solo, or to do a recitation is a way of satisfying this need and being certain of winning applause as well. We remind the reader of the unhappy cantor who roused such antagonism with his continuous singing, and how his better adjustment within the group was marked by his willingness to sing on program occasions only.

During the parties the president and vice-president preside on the platform together with a staff member. The president is the master of ceremonies, but since he rarely

knows all the birthdayites it needs the staff member to supply the personal congratulations as each member's name is
called. Each rises in turn to be applauded and often to say a
few words. It is these comments which illuminate the meaning of this occasion.

Mr. Rauch was one of a large family which was bitterly
poor. As a boy he ran away from home and went to sea. He
remained a seaman all his life. He achieved a remarkable
degree of self-education with a strong drive toward social
betterment and social action, which led to his taking an
active part in various unions. Yet, despite these group experiences he seemed to be a solitary man who made few close
ties, never married, and at the center went only to the shop.
He rarely joined mass gatherings. When his birthday came
around it took much persuasion to induce him to take his
place at the table of honor. His name was called and the
speech he made was brief, ". . . I thank you all. . . . I just
want to tell you this is my 70th birthday . . . but it is the first
time in my life that it has ever been celebrated. . . ."—and
sat down abruptly. He later confided gruffly to a worker, "I
had to sit down—I damn near cried."

One of the Russian-born members also had no recollection
of ever celebrating her birthday, nor any idea of its date. She
thought it was somewhere near a Jewish religious festival,
and was given the nearest possible day. She claimed de-
lightedly that the worker had given her a birthday, and when
the following year came around she arrived with a birthday
cake for her special table of center friends. She had received
her first birthday card from her daughter who wrote loving
tributes on it in addition to its printed messages. She displayed it to everyone with radiant pride. It was inadvertently
gathered up and thrown away during the clearing, and she
frantically searched through the rubbish pails until she
found it, slightly damp, but otherwise intact.

When the members tell their neighbors of their birthday

celebration at the center and display their cards, it sometimes prompts other demonstrations of friendliness toward them. Thus Mr. Adler's landlady arranged a birthday supper for him in her apartment, to which she invited mutual friends.

Often the members' children or other relatives ask to attend the center party, and are pleased and perhaps impressed by seeing the status and hearing the tributes to their particular guest of honor.

Parties are sometimes arranged in a home of the center friends of a member. Mr. Edwards, who lived as lodger in Mrs. Henick's apartment, was the guest of honor on such an occasion. He is a bachelor who was born in England and has no relatives in America, nor, before coming to the center, had he any friends. But as this event indicated he became part of a warm circle, all of whom had family ties and pitied him for his lack of them. One of the staff workers was invited to this evening, and found that the group followed the center pattern for their entertainment—in table decorations, speeches, and singing—but with the addition of more elaborate refreshments and gifts. Mr. Edwards was completely overcome and in his speech, choked with emotion, said nothing like this had happened to him since he had left his mother.

These monthly parties appear to satisfy special needs of feeling, of the sense of intimacy, and are a substitute for the emotional sharing which family ties formerly provided. Since no matter how inconspicuous the daily role of any member, he too will be singled out once a year for special attention, all have the same stake in this event.

The center magazine has numerous contributions written by members about birthday parties. From the span of years we have selected three because of what they also reveal about the backgrounds of those who were moved to write about this subject.

1943. "I celebrated my birthday with some of the other members of the center whose birthdays fall in the same month. I am no longer as young but I am not so old. I did not have any place to go to enjoy myself. I heard of the center while sitting in the park. When I came to the building and inquired about the center I was surprised to see so many men and women playing games, talking, knitting, and crocheting. A young lady approached me and explained all about the center. I told her that I too could do something to occupy my mind. Since that time I have been painting, woodworking and doing other things. That young lady was Miss G. and I thank her for making me so happy. I hope to live next year to celebrate my birthday at the center once again."

Mr. Schultz. "The birthday party which was held on the 25th of January 1945 was grand. Eleven members celebrated their birthdays. Seventy-five were present. The tables were decorated in gay colors with beautiful flowers which Mr. Torman made. I had the honor of leading the march with a very nice lady. When we were all seated at the table a happy birthday was wished us by everybody. Mr. Sullivan recited a poem which he had written especially for me and I thanked him very much for it. This party gave me the opportunity to express to the membership what coming to the center has meant to me. Before the center opened I was very lonely. I sat in my room and looked at empty walls. I had lost all interest in life. I was not able to do any work. I felt absolutely useless, no good to myself or anyone else. Then I met Mr. Lowden. He played the piano and made me get interested in my music again which I had given up long ago. I have been singing songs here, and if I have given a little pleasure to some of you it has been a pleasure to me to be able to do so. Mr. Sullivan interested me in painting pictures, so coming to the center has given me a new interest in life. I no longer feel useless if I can still give a little pleasure to you, my friends. After all, why are we on this earth but to be kind and to help each other, and to give a little pleasure to those around us whenever we can."

Our last quotation is by a member mentioned in connection with craft work, the former foreign journalist who had been in a concentration camp and five of whose children had been killed by the Nazis.

1948. "Ladies and Gentlemen: I am delighted to see with honor all our friends who have come to participate in our birthday party. From the deepness of my heart I thank you very much, my dear friends, and wish you all to celebrate your birthdays up to one hundred and twenty with health and with many others. In appreciation of this party I want to say a few words in relation to our honorable committee. When a man is in the decline of his age, when he approaches the limit of life, he starts to think about his balance. Usually he feels a little morose, not everybody has children or family to encourage him to take part in his party, to elevate his shaky mood for a while. This worthy problem is solved by the center committee. The committee arranges for the members' birthday parties, cheers and animates them with these friendly entertainments, and makes them feel happy. Acknowledging the fruitful work, I have the honor to say to all the committee and to everybody who contributed to this noble work, I thank you very, very much. I extend my appreciation to Miss G. and Mr. Schultz, and those who are taking special interest in arranging the entertainment."

Throughout the ordinary week it is often clear that the center serves as a substitute for the larger community in which the older person no longer has a satisfying place. But at the birthday parties the frequent comment, "The center is our second home," supplies the answer to what family needs this occasion satisfies; to be individually loved, accepted, made much of; to share again in that normal and sustaining alternation between giving to others and receiving from others the expressions of affection and appreciation.

CHAPTER EIGHT

Music

Every item in a program has its own special benefits, as well as those which it shares with all other activities. Thus building a cabinet, painting a picture, or discussing political affairs will appeal to very different kinds of people. But all three will take on more meaning when they are planned to contribute in some way to the community as a whole—a cabinet for the workshop; a picture hung in the lounge, or a discussion leading to some constructive action doubles its value. Since the sense of belonging to a community is to the older person so important a background for all his personal satisfactions this orientation will be a constant objective for such activity.

Among all the program resources at our command, music occupies a unique place in what it does for the individual performer or a group of performers. It relates him or them to others since an audience is an integral part of the activity. But music enables him to reach the emotions of his audience. He can circumvent the barriers of language to convey feelings common to all human beings. Music can manipulate moods, can induce gaiety, sadness, tenderness, solemnity, can evoke early memories or dramatize ideas. By its range of appeal the performer can unite his listeners with him in a bond of shared experience more immediate than any other medium can provide.

This uniting effect is so clear that most literature about recreation centers for the aged is illustrated with photographs of people singing together. Photographers are quick to catch the appeal of old faces alight with interest and pleasure. This is the goal we most hope for in programming, to find a way of combining personal and social satisfactions.

Music can achieve at least a beginning of this dual kind of satisfaction under purposeful leadership, for the leader knows that these combined satisfactions will make up for many imperfections of performance.

It happened that the first staff member at the center had no musical skill yet a lively appreciation of the benefits of music as a resource for creating atmosphere. She found that one member could play the piano and several still had good singing voices. This was enough with which to make gaiety at the first birthday party. We have mentioned that this was in honor of Mr. Isaacs' 86th birthday and that he responded by singing a ballad which in turn led to a general "sing." The worker fostered this beginning by using every occasion to call upon those who then showed that they could play or sing.

Mr. Isaacs' ballad was an especially fortunate introduction to musical performance at the center since he was popular for many reasons. Though bent and frail, he was always willing and eager to take part in everything that went on, be it games, discussion, or a new craft. This gave him a special place in the group because, as oldest member, his warm, outgoing personality and active interests made him an admired and reassuring example to the others. He had been born in England and had a repertoire of folk ballads which appealed to all. One great favorite was "Grandfather's Clock" which he dramatized as he sang, to the delight of his audience who applauded with demands for encores.

Presently the worker was able to secure a music teacher for one session a week, and group singing was started. As always with older people, the beginning was slow, but certain qualities of this teacher appealed to the class. She was already known to some who had met her at a nearby settlement house. She had great vitality and enthusiasm and a strong, deep voice, so that they listened with manifest pleasure to any song she proposed to teach them. She reassured the diffident that a good singing voice was not necessary, that they were going to sing for the pleasure of singing, and made this idea contagious by her enthusiasm. She was quick to observe those who seemed on the fringe of the group and to draw them in, or to notice those who seemed to be rejected and to find ways of modifying the attitude of the group toward them. While she thus skillfully fashioned group feeling she was equally resourceful in her presentation of songs. She told the story of each one, how it came to be written, why she had chosen it for them. If it was an American folk song, she mentioned its ties or similarity to those from other lands with which they were familiar. Once when she introduced a Negro spiritual and the group was humming the melody, someone said it sounded like a Jewish song. She said both were sad because they were written in a minor key. She then used this opportunity to explain major and minor keys.

The group was no longer diffident, but astir with liveliness and interest. The sessions were great fun. Those who had sung as soloists before came with eager confidence; and under her guidance those who had been almost afraid to try were exhilarated at the effects of merging their timid efforts in a group.

Then she began a new stage of progress by rehearsing them for a cantata. This was a more ambitious project which involved a new degree of coordinated effort. There were also parts, both sung and spoken, but now these parts must be cued with the chorus. The satisfaction of these special roles involved self-discipline as well, for those with stronger voices or more aggressive personalities had to temper and modify their performances to achieve a balance with the chorus.

The theme of the cantata, "We Build A Land," was the history of America, the contributions from many countries which served to conquer the wilderness and create a new civilization on these shores.

This was another approach to cultural differences. The theme of the cantata may well have given these many foreign-born a new perspective and emphasized again that the center, like America, was a union of many origins. But while the music dramatized this idea, rehearsing it was an actual experience of being and doing together. If Mrs. Mosher was rejected for her heavy accent and because she could not read, her strong, sweet voice and excellent pitch gave her a new value in their group. Realizing this she eagerly accepted the worker's offer to help her in memorizing the verses in private.

This performance was to be the feature of the Fourth of July program. The members attended rehearsals faithfully or anxiously explained in advance if something forced one of them to be absent. The performance itself was a great success. The total membership was much impressed and their applause gave the music group a feeling of joint achievement and confidence.

Since then there have been other music teachers and more such projects. The subsequent teacher made use of their varied backgrounds to build up a folk song festival of many nations. From the impetus of the music group's activity and its monthly programs at birthday parties, many individuals found new avenues for gaining status, pleasure, and new relationships in the community.

Mrs. Alden was a timid, reserved, little woman, known only to the friendly circle of the kitchen committee with whom she served. At the time she came to the center she was under great strain from an unhappy relationship with a niece with whom she shared an apartment. But presently the niece moved elsewhere. Her relief showed in her change of manner. She was relaxed and hummed and sang over her work. She had sung in a church choir in her youth and her center friends affectionately urged and bullied her into promising to sing a solo on the program.

Mr. Schultz arranged this, since in their daily work in the refreshment committee they were in constant contact. Her voice, although not strong, was sweet and true. She was badly frightened at first, but her gentle prettiness, white-haired and brown-eyed, and the old-fashioned song she sang, made an appealing performance. Her friends were an enthusiastic claque, and Mr. Schultz, who was then president, continued to give her much support and encouragement. He began practicing with her, since for both singing had been one of the pleasures of their youth. Their friendship deepened as they discovered more interests which they shared, and as Mrs. Alden's self-confidence grew through the new status her singing gave her. They might have married had not Mrs. Alden been afraid.

Her first husband had died suddenly of a heart condition and the fact that Mr. Schultz had the same ailment made her unwilling to face for the second time the possibility of such a shock. Yet for the three years which remained of her life they gave each other devoted companionship, and when her own strength suddenly failed Mr. Schultz went to her apartment daily to take care of her and was with her when the end came.

Because music had such a wide range of effects, releasing tension, raising spirits, promoting good feeling, the introduction of rhythm bands has a special value. It enables many to take part in a performance who otherwise would have no means of musical expression, or perhaps find this the only kind of group participation which attracts them.

The musical instruments used at the center are rudimentary and involve only a sense of timing and rhythm, but with a skillful accompanist at the piano the combination of cymbals, drums, tambourines, and triangles can give a variety of musical effects. Observing the rhythm band rehearsals, one can see what is happening to the participants. Much bottled-up feeling can be vented in the bangs and crashes of these instruments, and then be tempered to a socially acceptable result as timing and shading are practiced. Moods change

visibly as one watches, bodies and faces show increasing liveliness, until after a crashing finale, there are broad smiles and
tambourines wave in the air.

Mr. Lauber, aged 75, is a restless, physically tireless individual, who has always been an isolate at the center. He is
not obviously so, since he will talk briefly and smilingly to
anyone, but he cannot sit still nor has he ever attached himself to anyone. Instead he preferred to run errands for the
center and would call at the office as soon as he arrived to see
where he might be sent. Yet the rhythm band captured his
flickering attention and he was anxious to join. Although
there were plenty of cymbals he bought his own, perhaps because he might find it hard to depend on sharing in the common pool of instruments. Now he attends rehearsals regularly, beams as he crashes his brasses, and seems delighted
at having a part in the parties or practice sessions to which
he formerly gave only a brief glance during his comings and
goings.

In the past years there have been only a few members who
had real mastery of an instrument; one a former piano
teacher, the other a former concert performer. For both it has
been an avenue of rapport with others which they used
according to their needs. Another member had been a violinist in an orchestra, but a crippling arthritis makes it impossible for him to play. At the center he began composing
music. He wrote a melody for a poem about the center and
set to music other verses written by the members. This ability, unique in this membership, has given him a prestige in
this community which has helped him to adjust to the physical handicap that ended his violin playing. Often when he
comes to the office for the music paper which we supply he
speaks of what a wonderful place the center is. Once a visiting
photographer posed him, pencil in hand, over his notation
paper. It was an excellent portrait and he was delighted with
his copy which he plans to send to his son. "Now he'll see
what they think of me here!"

Others play the violin, the piano, concertina, harmonica, or mandolin, often in the late afternoon in the lounge, where a cluster of those sitting nearby may sing, or a few couples dance to the tunes.

We have barely touched the surface of what music can do for older people. There have been moments when it produced group effects that seemed almost magical in their speed and completeness; when its power to change moods by evoking emotion, lifted a roomful of people out of their personal dissatisfactions into sudden response and harmony.

One example occurred in the overcrowded lounge one afternoon. We have described the diverse composition of this room's inhabitants—the card players, the passive sitters, the constant flux of those checking in for attendance. This is a restless, noisy area, of groups generally indifferent to each other, often critical and hostile when overcrowding and too many voices affect tempers.

It often happens that near the end of the day some one plays the piano, and while the card players vigorously protest against the disturbance of a television program, they accept piano music. One day a man stood beside the piano to sing in Russian, the Volga Boat Song. Many in that large room came from Russia and there was sudden quiet. As the performance reached the second verse, out of the silence a low chorus began, some softly singing the Russian words, others humming the familiar melody. The sad, rhythmic song gathered volume from all parts of the room, swelling to the end, followed by a crash of applause.

CHAPTER NINE

Dramatics

As the center grew in membership new projects suggested themselves and were added to the program in an effort to increase the range of experiences offered by this community. By now it was abundantly clear to the staff that the center was supplying a whole pattern of living, be it active or passive, to those who were using it daily. Therefore more interests must constantly be explored for what enrichment they might offer. Indeed the term "recreation center" so naively used at first, for some time had seemed inadequate to cover the evolving objectives of such an institution as each year highlighted new needs and suggested new experiments and services.

That the schedule of activities was being used by some as a substitute for their former work days was not merely a staff interpretation. It was artlessly confirmed by a member who came daily and was involved in many special interest groups. She came to ask us to arrange her transportation to a hobby show, because, as she said eagerly, she would love to go as she never went anywhere for recreation.

The range of program activities is determined by many factors: skillful leadership, enough space to permit each group to meet in privacy, sometimes special equipment and funds for materials. But the most important prerequisite is imagination—a staff personnel which can recognize the latent possibilities of interest and develop them into new and fruitful experiences and has the patience and skill to adapt the tempo of learning to the level of the group.

Four years ago a dramatics group was organized. At that time many of its participants had already had various kinds of group experience. But this project, which involved writing, producing, costuming and acting in a play, was a more complex goal of group activity than any that had yet been attempted. It would call for a new level of group co-operation since the final success depended on the effective performance of each participant. Moreover, unlike most other projects, the satisfaction of achievement lay far in the future. The final goal of public performance necessitated many months of preparation, of efforts which had to be sustained through progressive stages of improvement. It was, therefore, an extended learning process of increasingly integrated performance and consequently of continuously developing interrelationships between the participants. But since all groups are also in constant interaction with the rest of the center community, the effects of the dramatics club's achievement were not confined to that group alone. A public performance, which most of the center's members attended, gave them a feeling that the club itself had achieved a new status. Newspaper and radio comments, the interest of relatives, friends and neighbors who came to see the play, all contributed to this feeling of the club's importance.

For these reasons this project was also a milestone in the community's development, its effects spreading to and influencing many more than the actual participants. We would like to condense some of the stages of this venture, since both within the active group and in the project's effects on total membership there was a process of growth and learning and change greater than could be foreseen when it was first undertaken.

With one exception, the members who assembled for that first planning session had had no experience in acting, save two who had taken part in some amateur theatricals many years before. The nearest equivalent to performing to an audience was a pseudo-radio skit, given at the center the year before, but then the parts were written by the staff and read by the participants.

The exception was a man whose acute need to win recognition in this community had been one of the immediate reasons for thinking of dramatics. Mr. Edwards has been mentioned before as the Englishman, aged 70, who came to the center when convalescing from a stroke, who had neither family nor friends in this country and who was elected secretary because of his superior diction and platform manner. When his term of office ended he became a candidate for the presidency. He was defeated in the election, and was profoundly shaken and bitter over this disappointment. Though he took part in several special interest groups, none of them satisfied his craving for conspicuous status. In the poetry group he showed intense rivalry with its leader, Mr. Sullivan. He painted, but his skill was inferior to that of other members of the art group. His physical limitations curtailed his efforts when he tried woodcraft and while he took part in the music sessions he was not outstanding. But as a young man he had worked as a stage hand and in later years had taken part in amateur theatricals. He had always wanted to be an actor and felt that he knew more about dramatics than anyone at the center.

During the post-election period, when his own emotional upset fed an undercurrent of disturbed feelings in the membership, it seemed timely to introduce a new program feature and the dramatics group was organized.

Mr. Edwards was ablaze with ambition to excel in this activity and spoke to many members about the project, claiming that in his youth he had had wide experience both in acting and in producing plays. He even bought the script of a play which he felt would be suitable for the members to produce. While his enthusiasm was helpful in stimulating interest in this innovation, the staff's objective was to find a vehicle by means of which the maximum number of people could participate and which did not involve the memorizing of long parts. Indeed, at this time, as in the previous year when the radio script had been given, the staff assumed that there would be difficulty in memorizing. This assumption was later to be proven wrong as the interest of the participants intensified.

There was a second key figure in this project, Mr. Schultz, who in time was to assist and even take over much of the direction of the play, and to be accepted by the group in this role. He differed from Mr. Edwards in almost every trait. He had been at the center since its inception and has been mentioned often in this report, as the first vice-president and in connection with many other activities. He had poise and inner security, and while the center is as important to him as to Mr. Edwards, since he too is alone in the world, his activities there have always maintained a sound balance between giving service to the community and doing things which satisfy his personal needs. He was at this time in charge of the entertainment programs and served daily as waiter for the refreshments. His excellent singing voice made him an outstanding member of the music group and he was one of the first to join the art class. His pictures had considerable success and seven were sold at the annual bazaar. Finally, it was he who had been elected president in the elections which shortly preceded the experiment in dramatics. Therefore, the records of this group's progress toward the goal of performance will also be a close-up view of how Mr. Edwards' hostility toward his successful rival changed to cooperation with him, and the successive stages of that change.

The project was put in charge of a male student from a school of social work, as part of his field training at the center.

Twenty-two members came to the first meeting. They ranged in age from 64 to 88, and were evenly divided as to men and women. Six were American-born, three Russian, three Irish, two were from Poland, two from England, and one each from Latvia and Roumania. Fourteen were Jewish, four Protestant, and four Catholic. Five were married. Most of the rest were widows and widowers.

The staff leader was introduced to the group by the head worker, though he had met some of them previously by visiting the poetry group. Mrs. Epstein said she was glad that they had a "teacher" who would show them how to act. He explained that this would be a group experience in which they would all be working together. He then asked them for suggestions as to the kind of dramatics which would interest them. One woman proposed short, original skits; a man suggested reciting poems; another, Mr. McCarthy, illustrated his idea of dramatics by reciting a humorous poem with gestures; and Mr. Sullivan said all must have had experiences from which humorous skits could be made "to cheer old people up."

Several members expressed the fear that old people could not memorize long parts and some that their poor English would be a handicap. The worker then repeated that this would be a group experience in which everyone would have a role that would not be too difficult. Some might perhaps use gestures without words; others act as prompters or stagehands. He told about dramatic workshops in which all phases of putting on a play are learned. Before the session ended he asked how often they wanted to meet and they decided once a week, choosing the day and the hour.

The worker records that many of these older people seem to join each new activity not primarily because they have a real interest in it, nor even a clear idea of what they hope to gain from it, but because of their need to be in every group.

In order to clarify their ideas about this activity, the staff leader first asked the group for their suggestions as to the kind of acting they wanted to do. This gave him a view of the range and type of their ideas in regard to what drama meant to them. It also exposed some of the hesitations and fears of various individuals about their ability to take part. His reassurance that there would be parts for all which they could fill, followed by his explanation of the workshop idea which makes use of other abilities besides acting, stilled some of these doubts.

In this first meeting his task was also to win their acceptance as leader as well as to demonstrate the character of their mutual relationship. He made it clear both by his words and his actions that he and they were working together as active participants, not as passive pupils learning from a teacher. He likewise established his relationship to Mr. Edwards as one of cooperation and not rivalry.

2nd Meeting.   The worker asked the members what dramatic incidents they might have experienced in their own lives. Eight members volunteered such episodes, ranging from riding on an elephant, being on a small boat in a storm, the anxiety of being separated from a husband during the subway rush, to a characteristic tale of his boyhood given by Mr. McCarthy when he tried to sneak into a circus tent and was booted by the guard right into the place he was trying to reach. The worker then recalled their suggestion of original skits and asked whether they might not do one on the center. This suggestion met with instant approval. There was great enthusiasm over the idea of using an experience in which they had all shared. Mr. Forman asked how soon it could be presented. The worker explained the need for a script and rehearsals. Mr. Edwards had written a narrative poem about the center. The worker had discussed this poem with him before the meeting and now suggested that they might make use of it as a starting point. Mr. Schultz suggested that they might use it as an outline to write scenes and dialogue "as we go along."

The meeting ended with the plan that Mr. Edwards and the worker go over the narrative and be ready to present it at the next meeting. The members were told that many of them appeared as characters in the poem and that there would be other parts which were impersonations of staff members and founders of the center.

In this meeting the worker was trying to develop in the group a concept of drama. He did so by calling on them to relate bits of personal history. This served the purpose of having each give an illustration of episodes which he considered dramatic. At the same time it was a means of having each one contribute to the goal of the meeting—to develop the next steps—and so begin the feeling of group cooperation.

In regard to a script, the worker's task was to find a vehicle by which their first experience in acting could be built around a common interest and their experiences at the center was the most natural choice. Moreover, by using Mr. Edwards' poem as a point of departure it gave him the sense of making a major contribution. It also gave an opportunity to all the others to feel that they could share in this theme. Within this framework, the action, development and characters might be flexibly expanded according to the capacities of the group. The head worker, with whom the leader had discussed this plan, also foresaw the possibility of developing this theme in such a way that if members dropped out because of illness or other reasons, the meaning of the play would not be affected. Likewise, parts could be added as others were drawn into participation. If individuals in the group wanted more lines, these were easily added. Lastly, this flexible structure made it possible to do without understudies and thus protect members from the gamble of rehearsing without the certainty of taking part in the final performance. However, there was still a great deal of work to be done with the group before this plan was accepted.

At the next meeting Mr. Edwards' poem was read to the group. In it the narartor meets a lonely old man in the park and introduces him to the center where he finds companionship and satisfying activities.

The worker proposed that the members write the dialogue of the various scenes, but it soon became apparent that this

was impossible. Mr. Darb was insistent that they had to have
a prepared script, and those who were asked to improvise
dialogue made long, eulogistic speeches about the center. It
was therefore decided that Mr. Edwards and the worker prepare the scene scripts.

This gave Mr. Edwards a special prestige which was to
serve him as compensation when his own great difficulties in
memorizing his part became apparent. He wrote most of the
first scenes, but as he and Mr. Kelly began rehearsing their
parts, he went through weeks of painful struggle to learn his
lines. He and the worker together wrote the dialogue for the
rest of the cast, but he also constantly tried to direct them in
their reading. They resented this because of his own poor
performance and told him so.

The worker helped him retain some status by giving him
credit for his writing efforts, by pointing out that his part
was longer than anyone's else, and therefore, took longer to
learn, and by rehearsing him privately.

This was a crucial period for Mr. Edwards, caught between
his desire to find in this project an outstanding role to compensate him for his defeat in the elections, and his difficulty
in memorizing the long part which he had written for himself. Under the criticisms of the rest of the cast he abandoned
his fantasy of being director-producer, as he saw himself
threatened with failure in his actual part. By desperately
concentrating his efforts he finally overcame his difficulties.
But meanwhile, the worker's support and the cast's enthusiasm for the project could tide him over a critical period and
enable him to substitute the satisfaction of group achievements for his former fantasies of his role, and finally, to
accept Mr. Schultz, his rival, as director and thus co-sharer
in this group success.

The script development was done by group discussion—
what activities should be put in to represent the center, the
episodes, scenes or by-play which best pictured its activities.
Presently the worker was doing most of the writing, and only
consulting Mr. Edwards before presenting the group with the
results. Yet he gave him public credit for these results and
thus helped him to maintain the feeling that he still had a
major role.

It should be mentioned here that all of the parts were

written in rhyme so that some of the confusion and lack of full understanding of the lines which were later revealed may have been partly due to this unfamiliar form.

It was during this time and while Mr. Schultz was leading the rehearsals of the chorus numbers, that he also began unobtrusively to assist in the directing. He did so calmly and without coercion and was accepted by the group. His own part was short and he had quickly memorized it.

Throughout the next meeting the scripts of the first and second acts were completed, and the members cast for their parts. The casting involved little selectivity, since, with the few exceptions to be mentioned later, everyone played himself in the activities which were habitual to him.

But two dramatic conceptions proved to be extremely difficult for the group to grasp. The first was that of accepting symbolic characters in the play to typify the activities of the center. They played themselves literaly and were capable of being hurt, offended or worried if a word or a reference in their lines seemed to depart from their picture of themselves or their actual relationship to someone else.

The other difficulty lay in impersonating others, in particular, the head worker who occurred in the play. At the beginning they even assumed that she herself would play the role. Only after having been reminded of the make-believe games of their childhood did one woman finally consent to take this part.

It is not clear just what caused this difficulty. It may have been due to the special feeling which all of the original members had toward the head worker. For several years she had been the only staff at the center, toward whom they had shown not only great affection but also great dependence. Therefore it needed the reminder of make-believe to lessen an inhibition against identifying with her.

Other impersonations which the script necessitated were

much more readily accepted. Mr. Darb, who was to represent the art teacher, had no hesitation in doing so. He was very pleased with his painting lessons and identification with the artist who taught him was a satisfying role. So also was Mr. Forman quite at ease in representing the wood worker.

When we compare the early stages of this dramatics project with the stages of producing a new play today the contrast is striking. Recent plays have shown a flexibility of imagination, an understanding of theme development, and characterization of roles which seemed beyond the comprehension of that first group. Again there is the factor that today the group has been augmented by more capable individuals. But the core of the early group is still active, and it was they who acquired at the slow pace which these sessions record, these dramatic skills, combined with the still more fundamental experience of working together in sustained cooperation.

By the next meeting the worker records that the discussions, comments, and suggestions were now fully focused on the play and no longer on alternatives. He felt a growing "we" feeling in the group in that there were no absences and lively participation in each stage of planning. They were also objecting to the presence of onlookers and demanded that only those in the play be allowed in the room during rehearsals. The seating arrangements in the scenes had brought together members who had either had little contact previously or had actively disliked each other. But it is notable that these antagonisms disappeared in the intense interest in this activity.

By the ninth rehearsal there was much mutual criticism of each other's performance, this one was speaking too fast, that one exaggerating his effects, etc. Yet these comments were not resented but accepted as contributions to their joint efforts and followed through. By the time that actual rehearsing began, members who were in the first act were asking for more lines in the second. Some were added. Others were assured of further lines in the third act.

Meantime, the news of the play had spread through the center and some twelve other members had come to investigate this activity and to ask for parts which could be written in. But many of these newcomers were to find that the activity did not suit them for a variety of reasons.

Mr. Tree, though born in England, was illiterate, a fact he could hitherto conceal but which made him promptly withdraw when he realized he would be expected to read a part. Mr. White and Mr. Patcheck were too deaf to be able to follow cues. Mr. LaSalle found his defective eyesight too great a handicap. Mr. Adelman had written a play and joined with great assurance that this qualified him for this activity. But his pompous personality made him so disliked, and the group made this so apparent that he soon dropped out. Mr. Mannheim came several times, more because of his interest in Mrs. Gimbel than in the activity and soon left. Such withdrawals were explained to the group only in a general way and their reaction was that they were satisfied to have anyone drop out who did not fully share their enthusiasm for the project.

Throughout this period, while the play was being developed between rehearsals, parts assigned during sessions, and changes being made as the group gained or lost participants, there were inevitable periods of lagging interest. The worker was dealing with a group whose level of capacity in acting and comprehension of the play as a whole was very uneven. Therefore his procedures had to be adapted to these levels as they revealed themselves, as the following record will illustrate.

12th Meeting: In order to deal with the problem of the group's increasing restiveness at the previous rehearsal, the worker explained what he termed the third phase of developing the play; namely, that the players actually live the parts they play in order to express all the emotion the lines called for. He said that because of the number of absentees they would test this out with the first act only.

The group thought this a good idea. As each gave his lines the worker asked him how he felt about them. Mr. Berger said he knew his and did not see why he had to come to rehearsals. Since the worker knew that he was one of the members whose attention span in regard to the play had been diminishing, he used him as object lesson for the group. Mr. B. had two lines to say, one addressed to the stranger who is being introduced to him and the second to his pinochle partner. He had been content merely to have memorized the words. The worker now explained the difference in direction of delivery and mood of the two lines, illustrating each, its timing, the accompanying actions of looking up and then at his cards, etc.

The group seemed to grasp a new level of meaning from this demonstration especially as Mr. Berger had real difficulty in following the worker's directions. Mrs. Chandler said, "We're a long way from actually knowing our parts, aren't we?" The worker realized that this new perception might cause anxiety and renewed insecurity and hastened to say that it was not hard to learn; that he would work with each one individually in interpreting their lines.

At this point the worker began to take the role of dramatic coach, drilling them in how to produce better effects. He had had to postpone this function because reading lines and keeping to their cues had been difficult enough for many of the participants. Some found reading hard, either because of poor eyesight or lack of schooling. But while some were reaching this level of adequacy, others were beginning to be bored. They did not realize that there were higher levels of performance, to which the worker now began gradually to introduce them. And during this period of slackening interest some of the previous hostilities of various members reappeared.

The finishing of the third act and plans for a prologue to be written by Mr. Sullivan served to rekindle enthusiasm and the group again worked well together. The casting had again brought together into sustained working relationship people who previously had hardly known each other.

Throughout the mid-period of rehearsing the worker was to exercise many diverse functions toward the group, other than only coaching. As the total script was finished he had to explain the significance of each part in relation to the whole. Thus, by keeping this conception before them, he maintained their enthusiasm for their joint efforts whenever individual difficulties or personal hostilities appeared. He saw to it that controversies about planning new features were made matters of group decision, thus again binding the group together whenever conflicting suggestions threatened to diminish this cohesiveness. He created roles for less capable individuals which they could fill. He revised Mr. Sullivan's part in such a way as might satisfy his need to feel that his special writing talents were being utilized and so helped to resolve his conflict between wanting to take part and his tendency to dominate. He was to discover at this late period that Mrs. Chandler, despite her aptitude for acting, had made little connection between her lines and the actual center setting to which they referred and to realize that her lack of comprehension was shared by others. This once more forced him never to take for granted their full understanding of any phase of the project, but always to adapt his guidance to their own tempo of comprehension.

Late in the rehearsing period there occurred an explosive episode precipitated by Mr. Sullivan. He, together with another member, had written the lyrics and music for a song in honor of the center's founder. He now announced that it must be included, although he had consulted no one about this matter. When it was pointed out to him that the music group and the dramatics group together must make such a decision, he was so angry that various members were dismayed at his outburst and began leaving the rehearsal. The worker's prompt intervention served to counteract the disruptive effects of his intransigence. His calm insistence that the group must determine where and when the song be used acted as supportive influence by which their departure was stopped; they were enabled to manifest their disapproval of Mr. Sullivan's behavior and by so doing, finally to force him into working in cooperation with the group.

For the following meeting the group had been offered the use of a nearby auditorium which had a stage. The report of this meeting is of interest because it records a new departure in the worker's methods with the group. There had been increasing restlessness and inattentiveness during rehearsals which he felt were due to the participants' slow progress toward better levels of performance. Therefore he decided to impose limitations on their conduct. The record seems to show that this one instance of an authoritarian role was accepted by the group.

The group met at the Maynard Studio where the worker asked them to begin by sitting in the audience. He planned in this way to give them the audience view of the stage so that they might picture how they would look and how they should place themselves in order to give the effects they intended. He then asked the first act cast to arrange themselves in their places on the stage. It was striking that only Mr. Darb, Mr. Cooper, Mrs. Barton and Mrs. Carter could do so in this new setting. The others did not know what to do with themselves. The worker then arranged each group and the play was begun. Much time was spent in showing Mr. Edwards and Mr. Kelly where they should stand and how they should act in the first scene which they do alone.

During this period there was much restlessness and talking. The worker now decided to impose a degree of discipline which he had never used before. He stopped the rehearsal to say, "If we are going to put on a play, someone has to be responsible for putting it together. If I am to be that person, then you are going to have to observe some rules of conduct during the rehearsal. If you are not able to or willing to cooperate in this manner, then the question arises whether or not we should continue."

The effect was startling. There was dead silence. The worker let it prolong itself until Mrs. Rossman said, "Mr. R., we know what you mean and we'll do our part." Mrs. Marcus said, "I don't see why it is necessary for him to tell you this at each rehearsal. If you don't want to do what is right, why don't you get out?" Mr. Edwards said, "He is right. You can't rehearse a play unless you have complete cooperation."

To soften the effect of his speech the worker explained to the group that as long as they were on the stage they were acting. If they were not listening carefully at each rehearsal they would miss their cues. They would therefore not progress but lose ground at each rehearsal, would become increasingly unsure of themselves and on the night of the play might be completely confused.

The group listened intently to this explanation, and from their expressions it made an impression and was to some a new train of thought.

During the second act the effects of the worker's authoritarian statements persisted. The group listened to his every word. Everyone was competing to please and to do his best in order to win his approval. He gave it constantly through a friendly nod, a pat on the back, an affirmative smile or a word of praise.

When members were not on the stage they sat in the audience. Such was the group cooperation at this point that the rejected Mrs. Horowitz was able to admonish Mrs. Marcus to be quiet, and be instantly obeyed though the latter is usually her constant critic. There was also much evidence of constant enjoyment of this activity, since each rehearsal was punctuated by funny or novel experiences for various individuals.

This rehearsal coincided with the termination of the student worker's period at the center, and although he had been sure that he could continue with the group in his leisure time, other commitments made this impossible. They were upset when they learned that he would be unable to continue with them and felt that he had let them down. A month was to elapse before another staff member could be assigned to this activity and it was noteworthy that although they were deeply disappointed by the worker's failure to return, the group was nevertheless now so welded together that they were able to continue rehearsals regularly under Mr. Schultz's direction. Perhaps his leadership at this moment when they were deprived of the worker served to peg their group confidence which had increased steadily since that first fumbling session. They attended his rehearsals faithfully. But when several members of the cast became ill the group showed real anxiety about the performance and insisted that the head worker arrange a date with the settlement house which was to make its auditorium available. They commented, "We can't go on rehearsing forever; too many people might get sick or drop out and the whole thing might be a failure."

The next worker was welcomed by the group. She was known to many of the cast from her other activities in the center and thus was easily acceptable to them. Her functions for the period between now and the final performance were to coach and to help them with the many decisions in regard to the arrangements for the play's performance. Most of them had mastered their lines and by now the concept of the play as a whole, which had been grasped so slowly, was clear to all. Therefore they were prepared to understand the objectives of her coaching and to respond with relief to the feeling that the final plans were moving forward apace with their rehearsing. This was often clear in the atmosphere after a rehearsal when the feeling of zest and satisfaction contrasted with the previous symptoms of uncertainty and anxiety, during the hiatus of staff supervision. Even though they were able to rehearse by themselves, nevertheless the presence of a worker seemed to give a needed sense of support, as well as the guidance necessary in the final stages of preparing for production.

By this time Mr. Edwards had become engrossed in his part and was content to accept Mr. Schultz as director. Not only had his former bitterness toward this successful presidential rival vanished but their continued cooperation in the play finally made them friends.

At this stage, interest in the play had become so universal that further details of arrangement were often discussed and settled at the general membership meetings, thus greatly increasing the number of people who shared in the plans for its performance.

Thus in the matter of programs, the group showed a wholly new initiative in planning the kind they wished and in deciding that there should be space included for advertisements which they proposed to solicit. This was the first time they had been willing to go into the community to explain the center, and to ask for contributions to its work. The kind and price range of the tickets were also matters of membership decision, as was their sale, which involved additional members who then came in for their share of heightened status and group approval through their efforts.

One month before the performance Mrs. Barton had a heart attack from which she recovered only a week before the "opening." Although the staff questioned the wisdom of her taking part, she insisted that she was well enough.

Mr. Darb likewise was ill during the last fortnight of rehearsals, but managed to appear, although subsequently he was again ill for two years.

The cast was keyed up to the day of the performance. There had been a dress rehearsal the day before to which a scattering of audience had been admitted but on this day every seat was filled.

Mr. Schultz, who had a very small speaking part, managed inconspicuously to carry a script from which he could prompt when necessary.

Mr. Edwards was shaking with excitement before the opening but once his scene had started, did excellently and needed only one or two whispered promptings. Mr. Darb delivered his lines with great aplomb and although he confused the order of two lines, commented accurately that the audience would not know the difference.

Mr. Lowden and Mrs. Chandler were outstanding. His voice was loud and his enunciation clear, while her high-keyed temperament made her react to the footlights like a professional. Although some of the others had difficulty in making their voices carry, they all performed well and with a mounting zest which conveyed itself to the audience. This zest, combined with the novelty of seeing old people acting, as well as the propaganda message of the play itself, all combined to produce a lively response and there was enthusiastic applause.

It is difficult to trace the specific effects of any one activity at the center since many members of one group are also participants in other interest groups and all are in fluctuating contact with each other in the mass activities. But certain effects were clear. The dramatics group for a time achieved a unique status in the center community by the success of their performance and also by the fact that it had been profitable.

They planned at once to donate their earnings to the center and discussed with the staff to what special acquisition the money should be applied. After having been given several suggestions, they chose to buy a moving picture projector which was presented to the membership at a general meeting.

We called this project a milestone in this community's development because it involved, actively or passively, so many of the members, and because the activity for the first time involved the outside community.

Not only did most of the center members attend, but the audience included relatives and friends of the cast and of other members, as well as landladies and neighbors. Their approval of the production was augmented by the favorable review which appeared in the theatre section of a large metropolitan newspaper and an equally favorable radio comment. Therefore each of the cast, no matter how insignificant his part, gained status in the group, in the center, and with relatives, friends and neighbors, because of his share in this success.

The stimulating effect of this increased group confidence was already manifest during the period when production plans were being made in membership meetings. It was not only the dramatics group which took the initiative in planning to solicit advertisements for the program. Many from the membership at large volunteered to do so, though some years before the members shrank from taking any action which involved going into the outside community.

Within the dramatics group there were many effects of this new experience. It welded together into a strongly self-conscious group, individuals many of whom had previously not known each other. It began friendships which had not existed before, a result which is one of the valuable products of all group activities. Within the framework of that cooperative effort, even Mr. Edwards' acute rivalry could be superceded by friendly relations to Mr. Schultz. In the same way it altered sub-groupings of members which before had either been indifferent or even hostile to each other. It gave several individuals a feeling of greater status in the eyes of their families by whom they had felt shoved aside or ignored. Not the least of the benefits was the lively interest and enjoyment which dramatics provided and continues to provide to all its participants, for this first play has been followed in the ensuing years by five more.

In the year following the first performance, the group was invited to repeat this production four times. The last time was at the Golden Jubilee celebration of the city, staged in a famous exhibition hall; an occasion which they felt gave them and the center special prestige and recognition as a pioneer organization. As Mrs. Brown said, "This time we must do our very best because there will be all kinds of people in the audience and we must show them what old people can do so that things will be better for old people in the future."

Their second play was an interesting proof of their vastly increased group confidence. They proposed to write a minstrel show. To many of them this had been the most familiar form of entertainment in their youth. The staff was frankly not in favor of this plan, both because there were Negro members at the center and in the cast and also because they were not enthusiastic about the quality of the jokes and variety acts which were proposed. But the members told them they were "too young to know what fun such shows were" and voted to continue their plans. Although they greatly enjoyed giving this show, they realized that there were no invitations to repeat it. The next script was more original. It was called "Fifty Years Ago" and was built around their recollections of conditions in the needle trades as they had known them in their youth. This play was again received with enthusiasm by the audience.

These plays are now written by the members, the costumes are made by the sewing group, the posters by those who paint and the many other tasks of staging the performance are all done by the members themselves. They have come a long way from the first doubtful questions as to how old people could remember lines or learn to act. Newcomers to the group find the assurance of the original members contagious so that several conspicuously timid individuals have been drawn into this activity by their friends and after a public performance their increased self-confidence impelled them to join other activities as well.

It therefore seems sound to claim that dramatics has shown many of the results which are of most value to this age group.

It increased self-confidence, the ability to learn, to carry through prolonged cooperative efforts; it created relationships and finally, it carried the participants beyond the confines of their protected environment to again face the outside world.

CHAPTER TEN

The Non-Participating Members

We describe the program of activities which a recreation center offers to the older person and from which we hope each will find something to meet his or her needs. We watch individuals and try to help their adjustments to others; we try to supply sensitive listening and counseling when it is asked for. We record what we can of the process of these adaptations as we see them in groups and catch them in such confidences or in episodes throughout the center days. But whatever we report leaves us with the sense of the significant things that were omitted. No report can presume to have grasped the whole meaning of the activities, reactions, motivations and needs it records. All human beings are both alike and each unique.

In reporting on this selected group of old people, we, their juniors, realize that we have neither the span of experience nor even the skill to convey the true and living diversity of these people with whom we are in daily contact.

Yet it is just this lively sense of endless diversity which makes for the fascination and the challenge of working with this age group. For beyond and behind our professional attention to these older people lies our own deeper human concern. They are answering for us the question: how does one meet the last part of life? What are the resources with which human beings adjust to the loss of family ties, of friends, of work, of diminishing energy and physical handicaps?

When the center was started we often told the members that they were pioneers in this social innovation and that the staff was learning from them. This statement has a truth beyond the context in which it was said. If society has neglected the aged, now when we belatedly turn our attention to them, we need to discover much more than only what they can and like to do. Over and beyond this immediate interest we are viewing the drama of human beings in the later years, each solving as best he may his tenacious desire to create a satisfying life.

The staff and the program undoubtedly contribute much to this need for satisfaction. But we are apt to observe and record these particular contributions, and to notice by only a passing glance, other episodes and bits of behavior which reveal the intricate patterns by which each human being at the center is unflaggingly weaving his own scheme of gratifications, compensations and personal fulfillments. It is easy to give an account of those who made the most use of the program opportunities, who find a group of friends, go to music, dramatics or the rhythm band sessions, visit the sick and speak at meetings. In our minds they are the model members, models, that is, in terms of the agency's facilities.

But we have at least as much to learn about the later years from the non-participants. Unless we try to understand what their needs are and how they are meeting them at a center, our knowledge is one-sided. They too may come frequently and therefore are using the center to fit their needs. Lest we fall into the trap of thinking that activity and accomplishment and the resulting status in the community are the only signs of satisfying adjustment, let us sample other kinds.

Mrs. Grocher is eighty-two and has been coming to the center for three years though she suffers from arthritis which makes it painful to walk, has a heart condition, and her eyesight is so defective that she can no longer knit or crochet, skills in which she formerly excelled. She comes daily, making the trip slowly and painfully, to sit all day at one table, chatting and occasionally playing rummy with those who have congregated at that spot. Through the years we have pieced together something of her pattern of satisfactions at the center and how they contrast with her life before her Department of Welfare investigator, noting her loneliness, referred her to us.

She had been twice married and widowed and has one son whom she rarely sees. She has two sisters one of whom lives in Ohio. The other, childless and in her seventies, still helps her husband in a drygoods shop in this city. Both have been financially more successful than she. As she once said when the Ohio sister sent the other $25 to give her in small amounts, "They know I can't keep money. I'd spend it all at once."

The relationship with the shopkeeping sister is good. She visits her once a week for dinner and is given clothing and extra food to take home. But one visit a week was not enough to counteract the emptiness of her life. She described her small furnished room, just large enough to hold a bed, chair and chest of drawers, and said that after breakfast she lay down to peer at the newspaper and then would fall asleep and if she slept in the daytime she was awake all night. "I got so blue I cried all day and hoped I would die soon. Now since I've been coming here I'm not even blue in the evening, there's so much to think about." Once she said her landlady asked her, "Do they pay you to go to that club, you go so early and come back so late?" and chuckling she added, "I told her it paid me!"

The focus of her interest at the club is her friendship with a man whom she had met there, Mr. Adelman, ten years her junior and married. His wife is a housebound invalid and a mute. This relationship exposed Mrs. Grocher to much criticism, probably not only because he was married but also because of his pompous personality. Her sister's family seems to have accepted him, however, for he often mentioned with gratification what "high up, aristocratic people" they were and that they liked him because "with them I use my manners."

He showed much consideration for her, calling for her daily and taking her home, consulting her wishes at all times and submitting to her judgment. She in turn protected him against the criticism and rejection of others whenever he got into quarrels. Though she herself got on well with others she left her chosen table for months when the others there found him intolerable, though on the days when he was absent, she moved back.

Her attitude, however, was capable of great variation toward him. Whatever their private relationship she treated him with flirtatious condescension before the worker. This was especially marked when the unfortunate Mr. Adelman grew a mustache, indicating the meaning of this experiment by exhibiting a photograph of himself in his thirties when he was a foreman and which showed his luxuriant handlebars. She made fun of him for a week while he tried to defend the effect, until one morning he arrived with the adornment shorn off. During this teasing there was a sparkle and grace about this infirm old woman, an assurance of her feminine role, which at eighty-two again made visible another bit of her history—the sixteen year old Hungarian redhead who came to this country as a dancing teacher and "had so many fellows around I couldn't make up my mind who to take."

Certainly during Mr. Adelman's absences due to ill health she was never at a loss for masculine attention, but annexed it, and shed it again on his return with practiced deftness.

In her pattern of living three factors alternated: her melancholy feeling that she was a useless old woman who had lived too long; her ability to seize on this community to revive her specific feminine talents; and her need to be in daily contact with many people. Though she could hardly walk, all summer she wore a freshly laundered dress each day though the effort of washing and ironing them must have been enormous. The worker, to whom she often mentioned her "uselessness," introduced newcomers to her and told her privately that her enthusiasm for the club was a help in making them feel at home, to which she retorted, "So now I'm a one woman social agency!"

To her the entire program, except for the birthday parties, movies and general meetings was of no interest, yet coming to the center enabled her to fashion the pattern of satisfactions which meant most to her and she did so with a tenacious disregard of her physical handicaps.

If her only resources for meeting old age were her social talents we may cite in contrast the case of Mr. Blau, a frail old man aged eighty-six.

He came from Roumania, spoke and read five languages, and was respected at the center for his learning and knowledge of the Talmud. He had been a widower for many years yet often referred to his happy marriage. His son had died leaving him with a daughter-in-law and a granddaughter as his only relatives. The latter became a successful attorney and his relations with her were excellent though he refused to live with her, preferring a furnished room and "my freedom." At the center he followed a daily routine, coming late, playing cards for a few hours, making a little tour of the ladies with whom he was a great favorite and then returning to his room to get his evening meal and to listen to the radio as a substitute for the reading his defective eyesight no longer permitted.

What was outstanding about him was his patriarchal role. Younger men deferred to him and spoke of him with admiration and respect. The women responded with affection to his gentle gallantries. He had a lively and critical mind. He told a new worker that the center was the United Nations in miniature, where each reacted according to his abilities, some making the most of it and glad of its opportunities, others quarrelsome and critical "because that way they pull others down to their level and don't feel inferior."

But his attitude toward old age and his own adjustment were revealed in two episodes. The first occurred when he talked to a staff worker who had been trying to involve members in the special interest groups, painting and an embryo science class.

"You young people mean well," he began, "you're trying to

do everything for us and make us into painters and musicians and scientists. But there are things you don't know about old people; many of us enjoy not having to do things."

The other revealing incident came about quite accidentally. A newcomer, also a Roumanian, Mr. Morgenstern, had been referred to us and in the first interview spoke of his former success in business and the fact that he spoke five languages. He intimated that he could hardly be expected to find satisfaction in this kind of a social milieu. Perhaps it was Roumania and the five languages which prompted the worker to introduce him to Mr. Blau. When she did so Mr. Morgenstern was overwhelmed to recognize a friend of fifty years ago. They embraced and presently Mr. Morgenstern sat down to watch Mr. Blau's card game.

This was his only occupation for many weeks, but once the worker overheard their conversation. Mr. Morgenstern was speaking of the misery of old age: "When you're no longer successful, when you haven't a home and have to live in a furnished room, when you're in poor health!" Mr. Blau replied in real surprise, "What's the matter with you? This is the best time of life. You have enough to eat, a roof over your head and no responsibilities."

Here are three adjustments: a woman who feels old age as an intolerable burden if she has to be alone but who can find satisfactions among people; Mr. Blau whose seniority and personality traits bring him a satisfying status in the group but who makes his own routines of sociability and relaxed solitude; and his friend, Mr. Morgenstern, who can find no interests and no gratifications either among people or within himself. We need hardly stress how clearly in each case their earlier lives determined their later attitudes. But for the purposes of this record they are examples of those for whom the center has a meaning which is independent both of the program and largely of the staff. It is with the opportunities afforded by a community of contemporaries that they were able to use their resources, or in the case of Mr. Morgenstern, to find and cling to the one figure who symbolized his own past.

These three histories were selected from those members who congregate daily in the lounge. That area today is filled with some hundred members who remain there all day. These three individuals were described because their personalities and patterns of adjustment stood out among the others.

We would now like to discuss these others, the many who do not stand out, yet whose continued attendance over the months and years makes it clear that the center is important to them also.

We know that they come because being with people is better than being alone. We also see that once the habit of coming is established they may, superficially, seem to be completely non-participating. They tend to sit in the same places each day, chatting with whoever may be nearby. Sometimes we even discover that some of these individuals have talked together for weeks and months without learning each others' names.

Yet close observation throughout long periods reveals that there is a continual flux of grouping, sub-grouping and changing interpersonal relationships at work here too.

If we subtract the card players, whom we shall discuss later, there remains this large number of men and women who give us little opportunity to know them individually, who seem to want no special attention, have no desire to be occupied, and sometimes never even explore the other rooms of the center.

There are among them some married women who are housewives and who come in the afternoons "just to rest and see my friends." Others are single, widows and widowers with no other ties, who are content to spend the day talking together. Some are isolates who sit on the fringe of the group. In the social hierarchy of the center they have low status. It seems reasonable to assume that their status in this microcosm is much the same as it had been in the larger community during their younger years when they earned their living at unskilled labor after a minimum of schooling.

Yet despite their seeming apathy their daily presence in the lounge exposes them to the tide of activity which goes on there. They are present at the membership meetings where they hear the reports on all interest groups, announcements of future events, discussions of policy, reports of the sick committee visits and of any deaths. They will each be featured at a monthly birthday party. They will see the movies and hear the guest speakers. They will vote in the elections, will be approached during electioneering, will react to news and discussions and voice their opinions to each other. Thus, however inactive they appear, the center constantly supplies them with a variety of stimulation to which to react, in contrast to the monotony of a solitary life, and to counteract their own seeming lack of resources.

When we note the evidences of development and progress in the activity groups and of individuals in such groups we may feel baffled by the large number of passive members who remain outside them. Yet as we weigh our observations of this type of member through a kind of reasoning by contrast, we can make the inference that they benefit by coming. In terms of their capacities, their attendance is a sign and sometimes also the measure of their initiative.

That the center is important to them is confirmed by other observations than merely their attendance. These people show great uneasiness if their membership card is misplaced or lost. They will always report each other's absence so that inquiries will be made about the cause, or if they be ill that a "get-well" card will be sent. They will be sure to attend on election day no matter how stormy it may be, and will stay long after their usual time of leaving in order to hear the results. Once when told that a well-known physician was coming to visit, they waited until late in the afternoon, not because he was expected to speak, since he was not, but as they explained they wanted him to see a full attendance. These are all evidences of participation, clues to their concept of their role in this community as members, voters, representatives of the club; and shows that much is going on behind their apparently static behavior.

They are rarely articulate but sometimes, perhaps by accident, we are given insight into their reactions to this community and its influence on them.

Mr. Birnbaum was one of the isolates who came for a few hours a day over a period of several years. He exchanged a few words with some of the men while smoking in the hall. Otherwise he sat by himself watching and listening to others. He finally approached the worker for help in making application to an old age home, a move which his son was strongly urging after his wife had had to be committed to a mental hospital. He was apprehensive about the admission interview, depressed and uncertain about the future, yet unable to tolerate the anxiety of being alone in his apartment during long hours of sleepless nights. The worker gave him much attention and support, helped him come to a decision, and some days later inquired eagerly about the interview.

It seems that the son on seeing the institution had told his father that he did not belong among so fine a class of people and that his application would surely be rejected. The interviewer presently asked the son to wait outside and talked to Mr. Birnbaum alone. She commended him on the promptness and clarity of all his answers to her questions and finally said that his application would be accepted. When he reported this to the worker she said with a smile that it was a good lesson to his son and that our grown-up children sometimes still need to learn a thing or two. He flushed with pleasure, laughed and then became loquacious, explaining that while he was not like some people at the center, he couldn't get up and make a speech like they could, but take him alone and ask him things and he'd bet not a man there could answer quicker than he.

Here in the middle of the crucial problem of his future he revealed how much had been going on behind his uncommunicative visits to the center. He had been living in dread of the home, a dread which conflicted with his fear of being alone. This tension was exacerbated by his son's evaluation of him as being below the social standards of this institution. Then the worker's comment suddenly made him feel that acceptance was a disproof of this low rating and a sign of his adequacy. His self-esteem, sagging under the weight of these accumulated insecurities, abruptly revived and in almost stammering excitement he used this moment to redress the unfavorable comparisons of himself with others at the center which he seemed to have been making.

We give this brief episode so fully because a special chain of circumstances touched off this self-revelation of an individual typical of both the non-participants and even of the isolates. We considered it an indication of how much we do not know about these people and how much more it should be possible to know.

Years ago when all activities took place in the lounge and everyone could see everything that was going on, the worker learned valuable points about involving the older person in new interests. The same timidity and lack of confidence which at first prevented the members from speaking at meetings, volunteering for committees and taking the initiative in the simplest maintenance tasks, also characterized their reactions toward new occupations. The worker then found that one of the strongest motives for trying a new skill was not so much interest in it as the wish to please her and to be among those who were winning her attention, approval and encouragement. After the first beginners had made a start there was then a contagion of interest. "If he can do it, maybe I can too!" This interaction among participants might also work negatively so that those who began energetically might drop out as soon as others did better than they.

But the original motivation was a combination of personal relationship and exposure, a chance to see what someone else was doing, to have interest captured indirectly where a direct suggestion would only arouse resistance and quick refusal for fear of failure.

That was at the time when all the old people who came to the club were insecure and the club itself was in its infancy.

With these experiences in mind the lounge worker made an experiment some years ago which we would like to report because we believe it taught us much about the reactions and potentialities of the ever present groups of non-participants.

At that time the lounge had a row of chairs facing the entrance. This row was occupied by a group of men who, partly because their backgrounds limited their interests and also because some were infirm, sat together daily, talking Yiddish and apparently content to watch others.

Because this pattern of behavior indicated a segregation from the rest of the members, the worker made it her business to give "The Row" special attention. She began casually by sitting with them often and taking her coffee with them. She chatted of center events, learned Yiddish words and told of the clean-up jobs she was doing on closets upstairs which they had never seen.

Presently she brought down some of the materials from these closets and asked their help in sorting them. Then she brought wool remnants which she explained were to be torn into strips and rolled for rug braiding. There was startled attention and laughter the day she snipped and noisily tore up fabrics and even the frail Mr. Bacher began winding strips. The present Sergeant-at-arms, though not a member of The Row, came over then to volunteer his help and was pleased with her praise of his meticulously wound balls of material. Thus almost incidentally began his emergence from his card games to his present full-fledged activity. Then she began the first braided rug. At each stage of these occupations she explained the purpose of doing them; that these were salvage materials which we hoped to turn into salable articles for the bazaar. At the same time she used every conversational opportunity to know each man and to involve his cooperation. As the rug braiding got under way one man, formerly a tailor, offered to sew the braids together while others held the strips as she braided. He refused to try the braiding saying that was "woman's work." But after several weeks his impatience with her slowness in providing him with braided strips to sew made him experiment with the braiding and finally take it over.

Meanwhile, she had varied this project with others, fringing cloth for table mats, using colored plastic cord for making knotted or braided articles, making raffia brushes, etc.

The rug maker eventually left The Row and devoted himself with complete absorption to this occupation in a secluded corner of the lounge. Another man attached himself to him as helper.

But what was interesting was that before that happened the rest of the lounge came daily to watch these occupations and to praise The Row. Its members suddenly receiving this group approval and feeling a new closeness to the staff worker were aware of having achieved prestige. They began talking to other members, joining other groups in the lounge and exploring the upstairs rooms.

Of the eight only one learned a new craft which he continued with pleasure and increasing skill. But the passive helper began taking Yiddish-speaking newcomers on the tour of the rooms, induced his sister-in-law to become a member and has joined a discussion group which the lounge worker conducts. Another of The Row who had been a cabinet maker, began visiting the craft shop. He no longer wanted to work with wood but became interested in plastics, a medium new to him, and one to which his former skill was transferable.

This was an experiment in changing the pattern of one group. It demonstrated that the members of that group had individual needs and capacities which were not being satisfied by the behavior pattern into which they had fallen, but that they needed help before they could each move into other areas of contact and interest. Their grouping had been, as it were, by default. It also illustrated some of the stages necessary to change that pattern. The Row had no intention of making such a change and even less of doing things. They merely followed the development of their relationship with the worker, as she seemed to need help with her tasks. They responded to her attention to them by being glad to lend her a hand. The ensuing changes followed from what they accomplished and the reactions of the rest of the community to the sight of their new occupations.

This is almost a formula for introducing new projects to the insecure: response to the staff worker on a personal basis, welcoming her attention and interest, leaning on this interest to take the first steps in a new endeavor; then if she was skillful and the project appropriate, there follows a sense of accomplishment and a new awareness of group approval.

In this instance the actual occupation to all but one was only a means to this end of helping them to greater recognition and security in the center environment. All eight were stimulated into new relationships, however slight may have been their actual share in the project, and by the time that the rug maker had removed himself from The Row, its segregated character had ended.

Since the lounge is the place where all newcomers begin their contact with the center and where this kind of person may remain, these examples point up the special needs which challenge the lounge worker's skill. We by no means wish to infer that occupations are the desideratum for all people nor even that old people who seem content to come and sit, should be stirred into activity by zealous workers. Sometimes the effort of traveling to the center daily to share quietly as watcher in all that is going on, is as much as an old and infirm individual wants. Mrs. Grocher's case gives a closer view of how much fulfillment she contrived for herself, despite her arthritis, in just such daily sitting.

But a worker must be able to observe the difference between the inactivity of a Mrs. Grocher, which nevertheless is fully responsive, and the passivity of another individual who lacks the confidence and the know-how to branch out and find fuller satisfactions. Occupations are a device to help people to enrich their experiences in this community. Those who have the initiative to join groups or the craft shop, usually have a competence in the field of their choice which makes the activity itself rewarding. But with these "low status" individuals and groupings an activity must primarily give them a feeling of becoming active contributors to the community, for self-esteem is fortified by feeling a part of the give-and-take within the human circle. Once this purpose is clear it opens up an unlimited repertoire of things which can be made to serve that end.

This is a concept of motivation analagous to the one pointed up again and again in labor-management studies. When the value and the necessity of the least job in the chain of production is related to the whole, not only does it demonstrate that production depends on group cooperation, but the low man in the chain has been made to realize that he is a needed part of the chain.

Once when a new woman wiped a table the worker, knowing that this was her first spontaneous bit of activity, remarked that she had benefited the six others who were using it, and though this may seem an almost childish demonstration of value, its very simplicity was effective.

In discussing the growth of group control within this community and the standards of behavior by which it operates, we have mentioned the low rating in terms of these standards which is accorded to the habitual card players.

Members rarely comment on the behavior of the passive individuals whom we have been describing, but the card players are a frequent target of criticism. This occurs on various occasions. If there is a special job requiring volunteers someone is sure to snap "Let them do it! They never do anything for the center!"

Their playing hours was one of the first things to be regulated as the self-government officers began to take initiative in group control. In the laissez-faire days they had played throughout the refreshment period. Now a sharp blast of the whistle marks the midday pause when they must stop. This group hostility to the card players is interesting and some of its significance was clarified in two sessions of a discussion group which we shall summarize presently.

Card playing is a universal form of diversion and our observation of the old people who spend their days in this way has contributed to our understanding of adjustments in later years and of some of the needs which card games fill.

The players are mostly men. A very small number of women occasionally play together and it is then the simpler games such as gin rummy or solitaire with onlookers. Only in the last year have two capable and energetic women varied their many other activities by occasionally playing pinochle with the men with an obvious competence which made this social innovation another of their successes.

The players are divided into those who play every day and all day, and those who play for a short while and have other interests. Among the latter are some of the club's officers as well as many leaders in special interest groups. It was these individuals who, in the discussion sessions, made the most vehement and revealing criticisms of the habitual players.

Just as closer observation of the passive subgroups showed that their behavior was not static, so the card addicts also show individual differences as well as a group pattern which is in continuous interaction with the environment.

Card playing for men, especially when they are newcomers, has the special value of making the first contacts easier. Few newcomers signify a preference for some program feature during their first day of attendance. But while women find it easy to sit together and begin an acquaintance by conversation, men rarely do. To many of them, however, a game of cards is not only a familiar form of recreation but often the only form of social intercourse they have known.

Cards therefore are an easy way for the male newcomer to break the ice. If he wins it is a quick way of gaining satisfaction. Yet losing is not too painful. It does not threaten him with the feeling of failure as might other unfamiliar activities. If he has other interests he will learn of opportunities to satisfy them through the players. If he has not, the shifting combinations of players will extend his acquaintance of the membership. If he has language difficulties, he will play with those of his own background—Italian or Jewish—and through them will inevitably become more interested in the center as a whole.

This became clear through the changes in the behavior of the habitual players toward the membership meetings held in the lounge. On those days the players formerly used to leave or disappear to another room to continue the games which the meeting interrupted. Now they no longer do so nor are they restless and inattentive. They follow the proceedings closely and express their participation by applause or signs of disapproval. For they too are concerned with matters of policy, news of the members, reports of the sick committee, and will want to share in the visiting and being visited when illness may again isolate them.

Card playing, like the poetry reading group, may be a means of developing other potentialities:

Mr. Bachrach, who came in his late seventies, was illiterate. His card companions taught him to write figures to keep the score. When he displayed this accomplishment to the worker she suggested that he do the purchasing of center supplies. He did so for years, keeping his accounts with immense pride in their accuracy and by the time that buying was done on a wholesale basis, has today, in his eighties, evolved a full daily routine of other maintenance jobs.

Mr. Adler is an example of using card playing as a means of concealing problems of adjustment. He came to the center shortly after his retirement from work following an illness. His job had been in a home for the aged where he had been a capable and responsible employee. We therefore wondered if this sudden transition to inactivity among people somewhat like those among whom he had formerly acted in a staff role might not involve painful readjustments. Mr. Adler, however, showed no signs of conflict but spoke with enthusiasm of the club, said he was "advertising" it everywhere and for many weeks seemed content to be playing cards. A few months later he was one of a group of forty-five who went to a summer camp for two weeks. Here the need for taking turns in serving meals gave him an opportunity to use all his past experiences as restaurant manager and cook, and he quickly organized the most efficient methods of doing so.

This new experience of living together and enjoying the novelty of a camp holiday gave this group an unusual closeness and Mr. Adler's service and abilities were warmly recognized and praised. On his return to the center he then began to take over the management of the cafeteria. He made use of his former contacts to do wholesale buying, planned more varied menus, and introduced a few hot meals weekly which he cooked. Only when this activity was in full and successful swing did he confess to the staff how useless he had felt on retiring and how much it meant to him to find this new opportunity of exercising his competence.

He also introduced new methods of serving the increasing membership. There were to be tokens issued by the attendance recorder for coffee and cake, as well as the food tickets purchased from the lunch cashier. The new method at first resulted in much confusion, ill-temper and crowding at the kitchen counter, especially among the card players, as each one came for his own portion. He weathered this with calm assurance and announced from the platform that there should be a system of rotating volunteers, one from each table, to collect the tickets to be exchanged for the orders. Within a short time this innovation was accepted, in part because of his previous acquaintance with and popularity among the card players.

To many players the game has its own values as an activity —and not as a pleasant pastime alone. Outbursts of heated arguments now and then suggest that to some it serves deeper needs of the personality and that considerable aggression is involved in its competition. Perhaps to the addicts it may be a kind of ritualized pattern of aggression by which, in the alternation of winning and losing, a competitive drive is daily released and kept in balance.

Since playing cards is a universal practice among adults of many cultures it is not surprising that at the center it attracts both extremes of old people, the most capable and the least adequate.

We cite Mr. Feld as an example of the latter whose cerebral arteriosclerosis is progressively damaging his faculties. His memory and alertness are grossly impaired and in conversation he appears feeble, anxious and insecure. Yet he is able to play cards day in and day out and seems relaxed and happy while doing so.

Earlier in this chapter we spoke of learning about the adjustments of later years at such centers and of the danger of observing only those adjustments in which the program or the staff played a part.

Among the card players there are some whom we must not overlook. There are those who play cards not as a means of getting oriented in order later to do other things, nor as asocial addicts, nor because their ability to play holds up while other faculties decline. On the contrary they are well-adjusted people. They play cards as they probably always have, as a pleasant form of recreation, and come to the center because it is a place where they can find partners. There are several who come regularly twice a week for that purpose. Several have independent incomes. Like the housewives whom we have mentioned, they too still have a family life which furnishes them with occupation and relationships. They use the center as a men's club much as do others of the same age who are in more affluent circumstances.

Or they may come daily and play long hours. Such members are thoroughly aware of all that is going on at the center, understand the purposes of the program and are most willing and able to take on a special service to this community when it is needed. They value the center because, like Mr. Blau, they can use it to create a way of living which is not dependent on their families.

Mr. Florsheim has means of his own and lives with his wife in an apartment house in one of the better sections of the borough. His married daughter with her husband and children have an apartment in the same building. He was a textile merchant who had to retire three years ago because of a severe cardiac condition. He found it difficult to adjust to his sudden leisure. He was not used to being home all day and became tense and irritable with his wife. His family was much concerned and set about finding occupations for him. They asked him to take care of his grandchildren and to help with the marketing. He resented these contrived chores, not only because they were obviously contrived but because his family expected him to be content doing women's jobs. They heard of the center and his daughter and her husband came to see it since they were anxious not to make another suggestion which might prove unsuitable. They interviewed a staff member and were delighted with the work shop. They felt a hobby was exactly what their father needed, hoped the worker would be able to get him started and arranged a day when they would accompany him to the center.

The worker was introduced to Mr. Florsheim, an alert, well-groomed man of seventy-one with easy, pleasant manners. Since she already suspected his probable resistance to having occupations thrust on him, she spoke of the social purposes of the center, took him on a brief tour and introduced him to various men in the lounge. She had, of course, selected those most likely to be congenial. He was affable and seemed delighted to sit down to a game when they invited him to do so. He was well aware that his children had first inspected the center and probably had been told by them of the benefits of hobbies. Therefore the worker made no reference to crafts in the first few days but merely expressed friendly interest in whether he was enjoying himself.

She saw that he was well-liked and that he adapted himself
to a wide range of card players. She therefore commented
smilingly after a few days that he was on his own now, a re-
mark he seemed to appreciate.

He has been coming for about eighteen months. He arrives
early in the morning and stays all day. Once when he met
the worker on his way out he made a humorous reference to
time-and-a-half for overtime, linking his center days with
those which preceded the period of discontented idleness.
Certainly he looks far from discontented now. He is cheerful and has made many friends among the card players. He
attends the meetings and gives thoughtful attention to the
proceedings. He comes to hear any guest speaker. He signed
up for a course in home nursing and completed it, saying
this was knowledge which would be useful if any of his family
were ill. He gives faithful and hard-working service on the
waiters' committee. In short, he is glad to take his own selective part in this community. He did not need new skills or
hobbies to adjust to retirement. He needed another metier
in addition to his family where he could again be among
men and independent.

Some of the unconscious as well as the conscious reasons
for the community's hostility toward the card addicts became
clearer in two consecutive sessions of a discussion group.
There had been no indication at the beginning of the session
that the discussion would focus on this subject since the
ostensible topic was the center and what further program
additions or improvements should be made.

However, a significant comment from a man whose English
was very limited, rapidly brought it to this turn. He said,
"When you become sixty, when no longer you work, it's like
you're upside down, and if it goes on—if you're too upside
down it can make you sick. I want life shouldn't be like that
—I want here we should make it different." The worker
groped for paraphrases for this concept that retirement
should not mean a narrowing of life but a time when it
could broaden out, have more meaning, bring more understanding. His face lighted as he nodded at her translation of

his thought and the idea was quickly taken up by the others. But in a short while the group had shifted from developing its implications to describing the card players as an example of objectionable behavior at the center. To the worker's surprise the leaders of this group, who themselves often play, were the most intemperate in their denunciation of the addicts. From the items of behavior described, a kind of composite picture emerged. They had no self-control, they used bad language, they thought of nobody but themselves, they knew nothing of what was going on at the center, they should be forbidden to play a few days a week, they should be forced to come to such discussion groups to learn things, should be punished for their behavior; they were quarrelsome, noisy, abusive.

This image of a person self-centered, one-tracked, hostile and without self-control seemed like an effigy of the worst traits of old age which they were vehemently rejecting.

This session ended with their demand to continue this discussion next week. During the second session they returned to the subject of the card players but now there was a marked change of affect. They began finding explanations for their behavior, they did not know any better, they had not had much education, they were not as bad as they used to be, they obeyed rules and did take part in the meetings, they did not know how to find other interests, that the discussion group should help them to find wider horizons and share with them their own desire for further learning and development. There were many suggestions about the ways and means of doing so.

This is a condensed summary of the things which were said at the two meetings, but the subject matter aroused an intensity of feeling which was arresting. More people spoke than was usual and it was then rare for the group to demand to continue the same topic a week later. Therefore the change in emotional tone at the following session was equally striking, as well as the final recommendations which brought us back to the original subject: what further interests should be considered in programming.

It seemed clear that the hostility toward the card addicts expressed a dread of deterioration. They attributed to them all the worst symptoms of senescent impairment and then reacted to these traits with violent rejection. But the very violence of feeling they expressed served as a catharsis, so that by next week they were listing favorable signs of a growth process at work in the card players. By the same mechanism of displacement they then tackled the problem of how to prevent deterioration and, reassured of their own superiority, were recommending remedies for the card players' limitations.

Like the significant comment which touched off the whole discussion, these recommendations disclosed their own thinking about the later years, their own belief that regression or continued development depend on interest and stimulation. Nowhere else in the program has this ever come to such clear expression. To the question we cannot ask—what resources remain in the last of life—they were answering—there is aspiration and the creative thrust of the human spirit.

CHAPTER ELEVEN

Attitudes - Group Learning

Throughout this report we have been picturing the changes which occurred both in individuals and in the group-as-a-whole as the months and years of shared experiences went by.

We would now like to turn our attention to a specific area in which the changes were most noticeable, namely in the area of attitudes, and to discuss the role which the staff, one's fellow members, and the process of group learning plays in altering or modifying them.

When we ask ourselves why do people behave as they do, in groups or as individuals, we find that the question narrows down to an examination of their attitudes—that constellation of ideas, cultural influences, feelings, past experiences and even physical factors which determine one's approach to the happenings of daily living.

We have spoken of some of the conspicuous traits commonly attributed to old people and must repeat them here: intolerance of others, suspiciousness, fear of competition, envy, general insecurity; also self-centeredness, a tendency to complain or the passivity which indicates resignation, hopelessness, and a loss of interest in life. Most of these traits have been assumed to be the inevitable symptoms of old age without any further examination of why this should be so. But all psychological manifestations have causes and it is only because we have ignored the aged for so long that now some of the causes of these manifestations should seem a discovery to us.

Old age, we told our clients, is a new thing—as indeed it is in such numbers as to have become a universal social problem. Modern medicine, public health and sanitation, better nutrition have produced a new longevity, at the same time that machine industry demands young workers capable of speed. The older worker in a city is no longer closely knit to his community, nor even to a family home. There is no gradual transition from the former full-time activity of a factory or a workshop to an acceptably diminished usefulness—to tasks of helpfulness in the home or with the neighbors. In the sense in which it is true in small towns, there is no family home, nor are there neighbors, and the man or woman who can no longer work is abruptly cut off from the earning power, the sense of usefulness and the ties to his family on which, hitherto, his self-respect was based.

These are the social factors which share in producing the psychological traits we have so incuriously accepted as natural to the aged. They are defenses against the losses suffered at the hands of a society which sets no value on the older person and because of which he feels rejected and unloved.

Another factor which has operated to intensify this defensive behavior was the concept that learning ability ceases abruptly in early adulthood. It was not until 1928 that Thorndike's study of "Adult Learning" invalidated this assumption and opened new vistas of continuing development throughout the span of life. But the sterile assumption which it disproved lingers on in our culture and clings to the aged. They themselves, however much they react to their loss of status, nevertheless were brought up in that culture and so are also influenced by these assumptions.

We saw frequent evidences of that influence in the surprise of some newcomers that there should be a place where old people are welcome; in Mrs. Barton's comment that the Bible says man's days are three score and ten, and that older people should accept the fact of being on sufferance if they continue to exist beyond that time. It is significant, however, of the individual's conflict between culture and needs that she made this comment to the worker when discussing old age, as though in the abstract she considered this social verdict incontrovertible. Yet she in no wise accepted this dismal axiom in her daily living. She displayed the same eagerness to win status, sensitivity to competition, need for affection and recognition and response to new hopes and opportunities that all human beings will when their frustrated needs are again finding new outlets.

Another stereotyped concept about the aged is that their desires other than the purely vegetative, are diminished. This notion is a further alibi for our neglect of them and helps to account for the slowness in investigating their capacities and in working with their specific problems. These are three factors which affect the life situation of the aging. Individual worth is judged by productivity, capacity to develop is assumed to end in early adulthood, and desires are assumed to fade away. The effects of these factors on the social attitudes of older people were so damaging, that when we were confronted with the results, we were tempted to pool all the characteristics we observed under the label of social pathology, and to feel that no matter how individual his maladjustments might be, an old person's paramount need was to be among people.

This generalization had some justification. It gave meaning to our observations of one or two individuals whose behavior indicated that neither the program of activities, the services of the staff, nor even specific relationships to others were essential to satisfy their requirements. Sometimes just to find a roomful of contemporaries and to merge himself in their midst may be not only the limit of an older person's participation, but also the indication of his social needs.

Mr. Senior came to us because his sister-in-law, with whom

he lived, had learned that the center was nearby. He was unable to respond to a worker's friendly approaches beyond giving his name and address, yet he came daily and was always waiting on the doorstep in the morning a half hour before opening time. He would sit all day without talking to anyone. After six months he finally approached the worker to tell her that he was "in great trouble." She elicited the facts with difficulty: that he slept in his sister-in-law's living room, that she made him vacate it early, that he felt unwelcome in her household and did not know what to do next as he was living on a very small sum from Social Security. It developed that he had a daughter in another borough, who was contributing to his support and who, while she had no room to lodge him, would be glad to have him move to a furnished room near her and take all his meals with her family. The daughter came to see the worker to confirm her willingness and her affection and solicitude for her father. Moreover, the worker was able to arrange supplementary support through a grant of Old Age Assistance. But when this solution of his various problems was first presented to him he rejected it, saying "Then I wouldn't have the center."

It would, of course, be a sweeping generalization to say that the causes of maladjustment in the aged are social in origin. Such a statement ignores the constitutional factors and personal histories which form the individual, and which throughout each life determine the pattern of personality.

But just as psychoanalysis, by concentrating on the discovery of the unconscious factors which are dynamic in neurotic symptoms, threw a flood of new light on all behavior, so our observations, focused on the reactions and changes in reaction of old people within a community setting, gave us new insights into the importance of social frustrations in explaining their behavior. It drew our attention to the dynamic effects of the social environment in fostering changes in behavior and made us realize that the uniformity of some behavior traits were due to the uniformity of the social situation toward which these symptoms constitute a defense.

One of our first observations in regard to the defensive element in old people's behavior concerned their attitude toward physical ailments. When the center was opened some of the first people who came had been clinic habitues. They went to clinics four and five times a week, yet after becoming members these visits diminished sharply. On checking with the clinics we learned that their ailments were not such as could be much improved by treatment. It therefore appeared that the clinic visits had been used more for the sake of human contacts and their complaints as a means of getting attention than because of any physical benefits. When the center provided other outlets for these needs the ailments were accepted and the visits dropped.

We are all familiar with the old person in a family who daily recites a litany of his physical miseries. Yet such complaints are relatively rare in this setting of contemporaries. Within the family they are a bid for sympathy, an appeal resorted to in an unequal competition for an adequate share of family attention. With contemporaries, most of whom could match such complaints and where abilities and competition are equalized, the reason for such negative self-assertion disappears and physical ailments are minimized.

We refer again to Mrs. Grocher, whose various infirmities made her trip to the center a slow and painful task. Yet one stormy day she arrived with a heavy cold. When the worker asked her if it would not have been wiser to stay in bed she retorted, "No! In bed my cold would be just the same but here *I* feel better." She had clearly weighed the relaxation of bed rest against the physical hardship of reaching the center and decided in favor of the social contacts which meant more to her morale.

A short excerpt, taken from a tribute of one member to another, describes a change from depression to cheerful activity at the center. After sketching this member's many skills and services to the club it continued:

". . . One morning in February I met Mr. B. After our usual greeting I asked about his health. He was feeling low and said he felt like a subject ready to be carried out on a stretcher to the nearest hospital. I was worried and tried to think what we can do to make Mr. B. feel better. A little later in the day I was involved in conversation with other members when I suddenly heard someone call 'Coo! Coo!' The sound seemed to come from above. I looked up and there was Mr. B. on top of the tallest ladder silvering a metal lamp chain."

Many members comment that they felt ill on arriving in the morning and that throughout the day their headaches disappear and that they feel better in general. These changes are due to the effects of having access to a community, of exchanging one's lonely room for a place where one counts, where life again offers other preoccupations than one's physical condition, or where at least if one cannot wholly forget one's troubles, the ups and downs can be shared with others.

Thus the attitudes of self-centeredness and complaining undergo change through many factors; by a substitution of interests, by the tacit awareness that one's complaints are not unique, by the realization that self-centeredness leads to rejection, and that self-control and participation lead to the rewards of group approval and status.

The poetry group furnished much material which indicated a preoccupation with conduct and its effects in a community. No session passes without several selections that stress kindness to others, unselfishness, making light of troubles, etc., etc. These themes are a predominant trend and are more applauded than any other contributions. They may therefore be considered to represent an expression of standards of the character traits most approved. But these ideas are not presented in their own words. They are, as it were, selected texts on conduct and bear a strong resemblance to the copy-book maxims of childhood. It is as though these selections indicated in this age group a preoccupation with good behavior for which they draw on the teachings of childhood. But the preoccupation suggests the existence of strongly ambivalent feelings.

There can be no question that ambivalence of feeling is a problem. The traits ascribed to the aged are negativistic ones —expressions of insecurity toward life. But if these traits are reaction formations, which, as we have been assuming, stem in part from the trauma of losing status in the community and from being progressively isolated, then being restored to a community of other old people will not transform these defensive attitudes as though by magic. Only by the slow process of resocialization through satisfying interactions within this new community will attitudes against others change into attitudes of cooperation with others.

This process of socialization takes place on various levels simultaneously. For instance:

Mr. Shafter's paintings gave him a personal satisfaction which noticeably influenced his capacity to understand the English instructions and commendations of the painting teacher. However, when his mural was unveiled in a gratifying ceremony before the total membership, his identification with the community which had so extended the scope of his satisfactions was increased. He began to come to general meetings and parties. This one occasion, however, would not have been enough to stabilize the change from his former self-deprecating withdrawal from others. It needed the daily interaction with the smaller group within the craft shop and with the sub-group of those who likewise painted and were personally congenial, to enable him to form ties which sustained his more positive adjustment to this community.

Mr. Shafter had been influenced to begin painting by the first worker and for many months was dependent on her support and encouragement of his efforts until his own satisfaction of achievement through increased skill plus group recognition freed him from this need. This progression from individual support to winning status through achievement is a typical example of the worker's role in the socialization process of an individual.

As a leader in special interest groups, however, the professional role is twofold: to enable the group to achieve the purposes for which they come together, and to help individuals in it to find ways of participating in those purposes. Sometimes this procedure is reversed and the needs of an individual can be expanded into a group activity.

A group purpose was built around the talent of an individual in the poetry reading sessions which suggested itself to the worker when Mr. Sullivan showed her his poems and she wanted to use this interest to draw him into relationships with others. In this group he took a leadership role which was willingly accepted by others. His resulting status was presently augmented by his editorship of the center publication. These two activities have given him a unique position in the community. However, it was significant that for a long time his security could be seriously jeopardized by anything which threatened his exclusive leadership in these enterprises. For many months he was unable to share credit for the publication and only gradually came to accept a reorganization of other contributors into an editorial board. Yet his own editorials, as well as poems, have constantly dwelt on the theme of brotherhood of man as exemplified at the center—which indicates something of his own struggle with ambivalence of feeling despite his renewed satisfactions.

If we note such symptoms of struggle with negative feelings, we must again speculate on their causes. The virtues which the poetry group extols, kindness, unselfishness, making light of our troubles, etc., presuppose a large emotional capital of personal security, a working capital of daily satisfactions and sense of adequacy. But not many older people have such resources of assurance. The daily margin of security has narrowed. Life has brought many disappointments and defeats and if, in the favorable climate of this community, satisfactions and hopes are renewed, there must remain underneath the surface a constant, anxious expectancy that the compensations and fulfillments of today may not be sustained tomorrow. In this frame of mind anger lies near the surface as newly found contentment seems constantly threatened.

Individual attitudes are deeply influenced by the security which the group attains from their sense of joint achievements. Again the poetry group can serve as illustration. Members from very different levels of education find within its framework of performance and assured applause, a source of self-confidence through group support. However, if the value of this group purpose is attacked, each member's security, in the measure that he has invested it in that value, is undermined. At such moments there may be an explosion of feelings which needs staff help. We quote here the record of such a crisis:

Mr. Sullivan, with white face and set lips, appears in the office, saying that he wants Miss G. to come to the poetry group for a few minutes. Though she was busy with a visitor she sensed some crisis and excused herself at once to go with him. Walking down the hall she asked what had happened and he answered, "You know that chap, K.? Well, yesterday in the lounge he was talking to Mrs. Schwinn. She says he insulted all the members and the folks are disturbed about it." She opened the door to find the whole group waiting in silence. As soon as she entered there was a burst of applause. She took a chair facing the group and Mr. Sullivan seated himself at the desk. He then explained that he had called her in because of Mr. K. and did she know whom he meant. She nodded and he went on that yesterday he had said insulting things to Mrs. Schwinn about Miss G., about all the staff, and about the whole center. He wanted Miss G. to know of it and that Mrs. Schwinn would tell the story.

Mrs. Schwinn stepped to the front and facing sidewise to look at Miss G. spoke excitedly. Mr. K. had said that the center was awful—look at the dirty floor—Miss G. couldn't even keep the floors clean. She had asked him, if he found the place so dirty, why did he come here? He had replied by making further insulting comments about the staff, had ridiculed the poetry group, had said nobody could write anything but jingles, that Mr. Sullivan himself couldn't even spell cat, she had retorted, and finally he had called her a name—'which she didn't even know what it meant'—he had called her a Hottentot—she had been so upset by this epithet that she asked him why the hell he came at all, and why the hell didn't he get out?

Through all of this the group listened, closely watching Miss G.'s expression, which changed gradually from grave attention to a burst of laughter at the end in which they all joined.

Miss G. rose and spoke with a deliberate slowness which gave time for the previous high feeling to subside and permitted a new atmosphere to grow from the attitude expressed by her relaxed manner. She began by saying that one of the things which Mr. Sullivan had always praised at the center was the many diverse kinds of people who made up the membership—and that she too felt that this was a wonderful thing. "But," she added, "most of you who come here know what you want. Some of you come because you want to be with people. Some of you come to Poetry, or to work in the shop, or to sing in the chorus or to act, and you are happy doing these things. You are the fortunate ones. But some come here without knowing what it is they want—feeling they want something but not being able to find it—and not knowing makes them unhappy. I think Mr. K. is such a person and I think he is a very unhappy man. And you know when people are unhappy they take it out on others. They deny that they are unhappy by saying that they are better than the others or by criticizing them. That's what I think Mr. K. is doing. Some of his criticisms are probably quite right. Our floors aren't too clean but we haven't much help or enough time. But if we have to choose between giving time to people or to floors, we think people are more important."

She continued in this vein to her conclusion "Why should we get upset at the things he said?" on a rising note that suggested a shrug. There was another burst of applause and much nodding, then one more question from Mrs. Schwinn, "What if he says bad things about the center to outsiders?" as though this were the last indefensible possibility. Miss G. answered, "People are smart—they catch on quickly—nine people out of ten to whom he criticizes the center will wonder about him. The members here have built up a reputation for themselves and one person can't harm it."

Throughout this talk the whole tone of the group changed —heads nodded—people looked at each other to corroborate their agreement. Mr. Sullivan's tense expression vanished and he smiled, as his confidence in the value of his Poetry Group was restored.

Several things had been accomplished by this talk. First of all the worker realized that the feelings roused by the "insults" indicated that Mr. K.'s criticisms had seriously threatened the group sense of the center's importance in general and of their own achievements in this particular group, a matter affecting the security of each and all. Their reaction was hostility and a desire to punish him by barring him from the club. Therefore these feelings were the first focus of her comments in speaking of the variety of people who were welded together here. She made use of their leader's frequent theme to make him the author of this observation, adding her affirmation of it to his. This served to restore what had been undermined, their group pride.

Next she offered them examples of behavior at the center with which they could individually identify themselves— pleasure in doing this or that, which further fortified their security. She then embarked on an explanation of Mr. K.'s behavior—implying that he was less fortunate than they. Their feelings now could shift from anger at being scorned by him, to thinking of him as the one deprived. Her evaluation of some of his criticisms was another way of demonstrating that the staff was not upset, and therefore they need not be, at what had been said, and that some critical comments may be justified and can be examined.

These were progressive steps in helping them to handle the feelings which had been aroused and by which these feelings could change from anger to renewed group security. She then added that she had left a visitor waiting for her but was glad that they had given her an opportunity to discuss the matter with them, and that before she left she wanted to mention one influence which the Poetry Group had had on the center. They had inspired the staff to plan a program of verses in celebration of the center's coming anniversary, that Mr. Sullivan had promised a poem for the occasion, that she had heard that Mr. Perry had written one which she hoped he would permit the staff to use, and that she especially wished to include Mrs. Waller's recent and beautiful verses. Since the latter had been especially hurt by Mr. K.'s scorn of her poems, and Mr. Sullivan had shown some feeling that Mr. Perry's poem was in competition with one he himself had written, this served to gather up all these productions into a joint achievement of this group which Mr. Sullivan was able to accept in his role as their leader.

She left quickly, again followed by applause, and the group broke up into clusters of eager discussion. In passing, the recorder overheard Mrs. F. say, "She said we should just ignore the whole thing. Well, I went through something like this here last year and decided to ignore it and am I happy now that I did!"

Some measure of increased security is derived from the feeling of the club's status and significance in the community and from whatever seems to enhance its importance. In the early days such relations to the community were contrived by the staff, through bazaars, through projects such as the toy making, and later through the public performances of the dramatics group. But as this experiment in work with the older person developed, the community in turn fed the sense of relationship; by the increasingly frequent newspaper publicity; by visitors from foreign countries; and by the frequent conducted tours of student nurses and student social workers, until today there is a lively conviction of the center's importance.

When the March of Time used the center to film a short on successful solutions of the problem of the aged, there was a stir of excitement. Those who were not included in a scene in the dressmaking department, crowded the doorway, and one man remarked with satisfaction, "Now Hollywood comes to us, and not a young girl in the picture."

Four years ago this group security was abruptly overthrown and changed into mass anxiety by unfortunate newspaper publicity. In an effort to stimulate contributions from the readers, the paper headlined its story with the threat that the center might be forced to close for lack of funds. The reaction was instantaneous and pitiable. People looked shocked and frightened and spread the bad news to each other. The head worker called a mass meeting to explain the intention of the headline and to reassure the membership that under no circumstances would the center be closed. As always, not everyone heard or was able to follow her talk, and individuals came to the staff for days to ask if it were true that the center was to be closed, and what were they to do if it did. Some wanted to take up a collection and assess each member five cents a week to help.

A by-product of this episode was the subsequent reaction of the Dramatics Group. With the exception of the profits from the annual bazaar to which everyone's efforts contributed, their annual play is the only group activity which earns a sizable lump sum. For some days after this explanation of the center's financial needs, they pointed out their unique value to the organization. The refreshment committee, which gave daily and devoted service to the entire membership, were upset by these claims and needed to be reassured that their service to all was just as valuable as earning sums of money.

In the early days the worker's role in initiating and stimulating the socializing process of welding the first collection of unrelated individuals into a group was clear. Her tools were inducing some to take over responsibility for services to the group, instituting self-government, fostering group discussions and decisions about program building—accompanied by many talks about the novelty of such a center and the members' pioneer role in these undertakings. This process of group learning could be accompanied by intensive and continued attention to the problems of the individuals who made up the group, to discover their blocks to cooperation, and to contrive ways to enable them to change their attitudes in order to participate more fully. At first their dependence on her leadership was extreme—as illustrated by their desire to elect her to the various offices of self-government. But gradually the group gained experience and assurance, and this assurance began to lessen the need for her active leadership. It also operated to influence individual attitudes. Group standards became articulate and individuals no longer conformed to please her, but to win acceptance from the group.

However, there were other areas in the lives of the members which at first operated as factors of difference to impede their group feeling. One such stemmed from their cultural and religious differences. The neighborhood in which the center is located has made its membership about eighty percent Jewish. The rest is an equal distribution of Protestants and Catholics. Many, if not most of this Jewish membership had previously had little close contact with Christians, and in their upbringing the traditions of both sects had stressed the differences between them rather than their common human interests. Now for the first time their needs were dependent on bridging these differences. They had lost their former ties to the work, family and religious groups which had fostered these mutual exclusions. Here was an area where staff help was necessary to enable them to resolve a conflict between tradition and need.

It was done in many ways and continuously. Wherever possible, religious holidays were combined. Christmas and Hannukah, Easter and Pesach, Purim and St. Patrick's Day made use of the decorations and the holiday foods of both religions. There was a Christmas tree flanked by the Hannukah lights, Christmas carols and Hannukah songs were part of the December program, hot cross buns and matzoths were served at the spring festival. These innovations were introduced by talks on the traditions of America, a democracy in which those of different races, creeds and color could live in harmony, united in the larger whole of being Americans. This made a synthesis of these differences which appealed especially to the many foreign-born. It appealed to their pride of citizenship in sanctioning the abandonment of prejudices. It did not erase them but it did help to reduce the sense of conflict. At the beginning this was indoctrination but as time went on there were spontaneous and genuine demonstrations of its acceptance. One such occurred quite early in the center's history. During the war years, when the price of Kosher turkey was prohibitive in December, the refreshment committee discussed the problem. "Mother Kelly" suggested that they serve non-Kosher turkey and Kosher cold cuts at the Hannukah-Christmas party, a solution accepted by all. It was also "Mother Kelly" who remembered to use separate paper plates for the matzoths and the leavened cake.

When an especially well-liked Catholic member of the shop group died, that group made a collection to send flowers to the funeral. But a Jewish member vetoed the plan, pointing out that the sum would pay for a Mass for the repose of his soul, which would mean more to his family than the flowers.

At another time, Orthodox Jews volunteered to serve as pall-bearers at the church funeral of a beloved Catholic member. To them this service represented a widening of social experience unprecedented in their younger days.

In this area the factors of racial difference and the prejudices which had sustained them were slowly overcome, as they usually are, by an intermingling which substituted real relationships to each other for the stereotypes of their earlier years. One might almost say that the extent to which an individual gave up his prejudices against members of another cultural group could be predicted from his capacity to form relationships. The more introverted the individual, the more he clung to such early patterns of segregation, and contrariwise, the more outgoing, the more rapidly he accepted the indoctrination. But the common need to find satisfaction in this new environment influenced even the poorest mixer. This was illustrated by Mr. B., one of the members of "The Row" experiment, when after many months of attention from a Christian worker he expressed his attachment to her by saying, "I don't really mind that you're not a Jew."

There was one problem in the lives of many of these members which colored their attitudes toward the center. This was the fact that they were receiving public assistance and their shame at being dependent on public support. After a lifetime of hard work they felt all their efforts had brought them was the disgrace of having to accept "charity." While they had lived alone they could conceal this fact, but many hesitated to come to a place which they thought would openly label them as recipients.

At first this matter was discussed privately with those who revealed their feelings to the worker. Her interpretation of Old Age Assistance as a right, a return, when they are no longer able to work, for the social wealth they had helped to create in the past was a new viewpoint and the first member to accept it made public her change of attitude in an article printed in the center publication.

Others who believed that the center existed for public

assistance recipients only were told this was not true. It was pointed out that no one was asked the source of his income, and that whether it was public or private, they all came for the same purpose—to be with people and to make new friends.

These talks were another phase of group learning and staff teaching which supplied social concepts that were new to them. Few had ever thought of their life experiences in other than narrowly personal terms. Just as a community designed for the aged increased an old person's self-confidence, so this new social perspective on public assistance diminished the sting of being recipients.

Another universal problem which could be helped by new interpretation was their relationships to their children. When their only remaining resource for love and attention was their children many were hurt and resentful at what they felt was their neglect and indifference.

Sometimes in asking the name of the nearest relative, the hesitant replies pointed to painful situations which later were confided to the workers. It might be any variation from the strain of living with their children's families to unhappiness at having to live alone. But rarely did anyone realize that his situation held universal factors and find the relief from personal hurt that this larger understanding can bring.

In a community of peers this painful subject was exposed to new influences. By comparing notes with others one might find general agreement that the younger generation were all selfish and neglectful. Or one might privately conclude that one's own children profited by comparison with others. But as counter-influence to this problem were the effects of again making a richer life of one's own with new interests and contacts, so that the excessive demands on one's children diminished.

This area of relationships to one's children may reflect the various stages of adjustment to old age and we can best sum up this chapter on the influence which group learning has in changing attitudes and the role of staff both in supplying new perspectives and in giving personalized help by once more giving an illustration.

Mr. Unger has been mentioned as the musician whose arthritis ended his career as a violinist. When we first met him he had lost his wife and had lived with a favorite daughter until she too had died. He was then living with another married daughter whose own children were grown up and had left the home.

The center meant much to Mr. Unger, not only because of his unique and satisfying occupation as composer, but as presently became clear, because it was an escape from the tensions of his home life. There were financial problems and his son-in-law, also a musician, had difficulty in finding work. Mr. Unger had been able, through his former contacts, to help him get a job, but the daughter was worried and tense and often vented her feelings on her father.

He had been managing in this arrangement by means of a small pension from his union and some help from his son, but now he felt a burden and an intruder in his daughter's home. He told the worker it made him miserable to have her quote the price of food items whenever they sat down to a meal and he felt he ought to move.

This was during a housing shortage and the worker decided it was wiser to help him to adjust to this arrangement than to expose him to the stress of making a radical change. She therefore pointed out to him its advantages: that he had a pleasant room of his own, well-cooked meals, and the orderliness and care which his daughter provided. She said that the rising cost of food was on everyone's mind—that in her own home prices were discussed at mealtime and that she did not take it personally.

She gave him another interpretation of his daughter's behavior toward him, why she made him the target of her bad temper. She said that when she was worried about her husband's job and their income, she could not risk upsetting their marriage by exploding at him. But a father was different. She was his child, and if she was tense and afraid of the future she could show her feelings to him because she was sure of his love. This conception made a deep impression on him. It gave him a new picture of himself, and his relationship to her to see that even her hostile behavior could still have its roots in her attachment to him.

The worker urged Mr. Unger to apply for Old Age Assistance but he balked for some time over one point. He did not mind becoming a recipient but he could not bring himself to agree to the requirement that he assign to the D. of W. his life insurance. "My daughter's the beneficiary and when I'm dead I want her to have that money." The worker asked him if he could obtain a cash surrender value. He said he could not. She asked him if he could, would he want to give that money to his daughter. He said, of course. She then pointed out that in assigning it to the Department, he was in a sense giving it to her in small amounts by reducing her expenses, and that should he die suddenly the Department would again assign to her as beneficiary the unused balance.

Though he grasped this point he was unable to take this step until another change in the home brought matters to a head. His daughter took a job and then found the care of their large apartment and the cooking of regular meals an added burden and talked of moving to a smaller place.

More furnished rooms had meantime become available and the worker felt that he was now ready for an independent living which he had never tried before. He finally made application for public assistance, coming to tell her of each stage of the procedure and at her suggestion, talking over his plans with his daughter. While taking these steps he was much encouraged by the fact that many of his friends at the center lived alone on public assistance and seemed content with their independence.

As soon as the grant was made, he found himself a pleasant room in his daughter's neighborhood, where he has been living ever since. It seemed a good sign of his new adjustment when he told the worker that he began talking to a man whom he had seen in the neighborhood for years but had not addressed. Now he wanted to get acquainted and they often met in a cafeteria to eat their meals together.

That was some five years ago. Just recently Mr. Unger sought out the worker to say, "You understand people. Something terrible has happened and I must talk to you." The day before, when visiting his daughter, she had asked him the name of his investigator. He asked why she wanted to know and she said brusquely that she wanted to tell her he ought to be in an old age home. He told her angrily that if he wanted to go to a home he and not she would arrange it. Their arguments were so heated that he told the worker he was never going to see her again.

But once more the worker could heal the breach. She reminded him that he had told her his daughter was very nervous. "Yes, and she has a husband who drives her crazy," he added. Then perhaps his visits to her "make her feel bad because you don't live there any more and because she can't have you there." "You mean her conscience bothers her?" he said with a brightening expression. "Yes, and therefore she wants you to go to a home where she'll be less worried about you because she knows that you'll be taken care of. She wants you to go there for her own sake, not yours."

He accepted this explanation, indeed his opening sentence in talking of the quarrel, "You understand people," was an appeal for an interpretation of their quarrel.

She added that while he did not need a home yet, it might still be a good idea to visit one and see for himself what they were like—since some years from now he might want to try one. He is now eighty-two, and with his daily visits to the center and his satisfying status in this community, has come to like the independence he achieved in the past years.

It may be objected that this was so clearly a case of prolonged individual counseling as hardly to justify its selection as an illustration of attitudes changed by group learning. Such extended personal help approaches case work. It is precisely for this reason that we have chosen it as an example.

Had Mr. Unger brought these same problems to the worker in a case work agency, it would have eliminated some of the most dynamic factors in his readjustment. It was the renewed satisfactions and status which the community gave him that counteracted his dependence on his daughter and gave him back his self-assurance in facing his difficulties in her home.

Likewise it was the example of others like himself, who were living alone which influenced his attitude toward achieving independence so late in life.

To make the transition and to accept these changes needed the bridge of understanding and warmth which the worker supplied. Mr. Unger needed to be able to express his hurt feelings and bitter thoughts and then to be helped to see, with deep relief, that his daughter too had conflicts, for to see them was to understand her behavior better and so to lessen his own unhappiness.

As he grows more feeble, he will undoubtedly be willing to consider the idea of an old age home, again because the community has shown him encouraging precedents of friends who have taken this step and are pleased with the results.

Case work alone might only have substituted dependence on the worker for his dependence on his daughter, and even though this meant a more objective and trained assistance for his problems, it was the influence of an environment of his peers which operated to release and to fortify his own initiative and to change his thinking about the readjustments he needed to make.

CHAPTER TWELVE

Discussion Groups

There has never been a time at the center when discussion has not played an important part in promoting community feeling. It served to focus everyone's attention on the purposes and evolving problems of functioning together. It gave individuals increased self-confidence, much as did dramatics, in being able to face an audience. It gave the staff a way of setting the tone in which community problems were handled, as well as an opportunity to emphasize the over-all perspective when issues tended to become too personal. But for several years discussions were limited to center affairs since it was the one interest which the members had in common. Yet as time went on the needs of the club widened the boundaries of their thinking and planning. It was at this point that certain attitudes of the members—the diffidence and insecurity so apparent in the first year, which had been overcome within this setting—were again startlingly manifest in relation to the outside world.

While discussing the sewing group's projects, a former tailor suggested that the members go to the local merchants to ask for donations of fabric remnants. He made the suggestion with eagerness and confidence and was upset at being instantly quashed. Someone finally said that as he was a rich man (meaning not a recipient of public support) he could try it, but they wouldn't think of it. The worker talked with him later, encouraged his plan, and when he did bring some meager donations, made sure that the membership knew of the results of his initiative.

A similar reaction was precipitated by another suggestion in regard to rationing during the war. Buying sugar at the chain stores involved fatiguing hours of standing in line and someone said that the stores should be asked to make special provision for old people to get rationed goods without queuing. But here again there was instant refusal to ask such a favor.

It was such samples of their social fearfulness at that stage which made their later confidence and initiative in soliciting advertisements so notable a proof of changing attitudes. The process of this change was most conspicuous in the history of a special discussion group.

But many things were happening simultaneously at this time. The membership was growing; the various committees were beginning to function; the membership meetings—then still held weekly—were reflecting an increasing know-how, and consequently there was a freer play of topics and suggestions.

The next issue which did carry them beyond the center concerned the adjacent park which many members used during pleasant weather. They spoke of the broken benches and of the boisterous behavior of the children which disturbed and frightened them. Someone suggested that the club write to both the Park Department to repair the benches and to the Police Department for better protection. The discussion now emphasized that as citizens they had a right to make such requests and the corresponding secretary was instructed to write these letters. Mild as were these demands they represented progress. To be with so many others who received public support was changing their sense of debased status and this step of combined social action had become possible.

There were differences in the types of social action which increasingly presented themselves, so that one step might be acceptable while another again arouse anxiety and resistance. Yet we attempt to record a sequence of such steps because through them we could trace the trend of further growth in the direction of concern with the wider world outside the club. Later this development was to lead to a formalized discussion group, but this was still four years in the future.

Another link in the sequence was provided when a member, Mr. Schulman, brought up the subject of Israel's efforts to achieve Statehood. This was a subject which reached deep into the feelings of many of these older people—men and women who in their youth had left behind them everything loved and familiar to seek in America a better future for themselves and their children. If old age had gradually narrowed each down to the small area of his or her personal needs and wants, the compelling vision of a Jewish State must again recall the wider horizons they had forgotten.

Mr. Schulman's suggestion was that the club send a resolution to the President of the United States reminding him of his promise to help minority groups. As soon as he finished speaking a Christian member jumped up to say that this was a political matter in which they had no concern. It should be interpolated that this member, Mr. Sullivan, had and has continued to have a fear of any topic which he feels might be controversial. At that, another Jewish member tried to remind the meeting of the six million Jews who had lost their lives in the persecution of their race, but he was overwhelmed with emotion and sobs choked his voice. The spectacle of his tears overwhelmed the audience with pity and dismay, many with painful awareness of their own kinship to this tragic history and with fear of what disunity this might precipitate here at the center. Some Christians, in an attempt to help the critical situation, tried to pacify feelings by maintaining this issue was beyond the scope of their action.

Throughout these stormy comments the originator of the suggestion persistently inquired were they or were they not going to send a resolution. The worker intervened to say that perhaps a small committee could sit down together and think this matter through and find a way of wording this resolution so that it might be acceptable to all. A committee was then appointed consisting of those who were eager to send the resolution, and those opposed. The worker guessed that the word resolution had a fearsome sound, that some were uncertain what it meant and afraid that they might be making some kind of commitment. She therefore came to the committee meeting armed with the dictionary and said that she wanted to be sure that they all understood its meaning, and read them the definition. It was clear that this relieved fears and set a tone to the discussion which followed. Presently one of the original Christian opponents, Mr. McCarthy, said, "This is not a political issue, it's a humanitarian one," and the originator, satisfied that he was not being opposed through prejudice, could say that the resolution was no longer timely and he preferred to withdraw it. The worker then asked whether she might be the one to report to the membership on this committee's discussion and decision, knowing that she could best highlight their achievement of resolving conflicting viewpoints.

The history of this episode illustrates many of the elements which were involved in the evolution of discussion at the center. There was not only the general fear of taking part in social issues and the ignorance and inexperience which made such procedures as a resolution frightening. There was also the dread of controversy among themselves, and the desire to avoid it by making politics and religion taboo. But we believe that there is more involved than the simple desire to avoid disunity in the club by arousing racial prejudices, powerful though this was on the part of the Jewish members.

For some this situation also involved the deeper, unconscious fear of ambivalent feelings, of arousing that latent hostility which, as we have said earlier, lies near the surface in so many older people and which constantly threatens to break through whenever something disturbs the pattern of their adjustments within a group. Mr. Sullivan's struggle with ambivalence has been discussed before, and we refer to it again because in such a crisis a worker needs to be able to sense the difference in motivation between Mr. Sullivan's vehement opposition, and that of Mr. McCarthy, a secure and flexible individual whose objection was accessible to the clarification of discussion. It is significant that Mr. Sullivan, though appointed to the committee, did not come to the session.

This committee meeting gave the worker an opportunity to guide the key figures through the experience of clarification, analyzing what had become an explosive topic, exchanging viewpoints, and reaching a decision. Learning this process of discussion was to take a long time, as we presently discovered when we attempted to introduce special sessions for that purpose.

As individuals began to know each other better there were many spontaneous discussions around the lounge. Sometimes the worker happened upon such a talk and joined it—using it to draw in those who sat on the fringe, or to build up the contribution of some shy individual to the development of a topic. These experiences suggested that sessions of planned discussion might be a fruitful addition to the program, and since a volunteer with years of teaching experience was available, the staff now talked to the members of beginning a discussion group. The first session was held in the lounge, to enable as many as possible to sample this activity, and the first topic was the purpose of such a group, whether they would be interested and what kind of things they would want to discuss. The date of the next meeting was fixed and the subject chosen was "Activities at the Center"—to be an evaluation of the program from the standpoint of the members, with suggestions for improvements.

That meeting was moved to the library and the volunteer leader took the chair. Sixteen members attended, among them Mr. Sullivan and Mr. McCarthy, as well as Mr. Schulman. Only three of the sixteen were women.

Nov. 1946.   The leader opened the meeting by announcing the topic and suggested, since she did not know the members, that they begin by having each in turn say what was on his mind. Mr. Schulman sat in the first row and she called on him. He said things were fine at the center, and he would like to talk of other things. The leader thanked him and proceeded to the next. He said he was not ready but would speak later. The next man said the same, so she asked for volunteers. Mr. Rothchild then rose to ask that the group discuss "England and the Jews." He added that he was interested in the subject and that he was sure others were also. At this, the meeting became charged with feeling and members began talking excitedly, several at the same time. Mr. Sullivan stood up at the front of the room and in a very authoritative voice said, "We're not going to talk about that," as if to settle the whole matter. Mr. Rothchild angrily asked why not. Mr. Sullivan said it had been agreed that there be no discussion of religion, race or creed, that the center was made up of many kinds of people and that it wasn't right to discuss only one race, though he himself "had nothing against the Jews or any other kind of people." Mr. Greenberg now pitched in and Mr. Schulman joined, so that all four were yelling at each other.

The leader asked all to sit down and tried to restore order by reminding them that no discussion was possible when people could not control their feelings, that the topic for the day had been chosen, and that she was sure they had ideas on this subject, etc. However, as soon as she finished, the four men all tried to speak again. Mr. Schulman started across the room shouting about discrimination, and the throttling of free speech. Mr. Greenberg was on his feet, protesting his right to continue the controversial topic. Mr. Rothchild and Mr. Sullivan were shouting about the same subject, the former saying, "Who suffered in this war more than the Jews?" and Mr. Sullivan retorting, "The Christians." Mr.

Schulman continuing his course to the door, turned to yell something at Sullivan, who, completely losing control of himself, told him to get out or he would throw him out. Schulman started toward him saying, "Go ahead, I dare you to throw me out." The leader told Schulman he was welcome to stay if he sat down, but he continued into the next room still yelling, followed by Greenberg, arguing excitedly. Mr. Schulman was beyond argument and went downstairs. Mr. Greenberg, at the leader's suggestion, returned and sat down.

The group was badly shaken by this explosion. One woman said such behavior was awful, and Mrs. Rapp said she had been in many discussion groups where the procedure was to have an informed speaker followed by questions and an exchange of opinion. The leader thanked her for this suggestion and asked for other comments. A man added that controversial subjects should be avoided and made a few soothing and complimentary remarks about Mr. Sullivan, whose leadership role he knew from the poetry group. Mr. Rothchild got up to say that he was sorry that he had started such a fracas, that he had asked the head worker to secure a speaker to lecture on Palestine, and had misunderstood the purpose of this meeting, thinking the leader was the promised lecturer, and that he would again discuss his plan with the head worker. He too added some pacifying words for Mr. Sullivan. Two other speakers once more attempted to discuss Jews and Gentiles, but were reminded the topic had been closed. Several others had drifted out of the room and it was therefore decided to end the session, though no subject for the following meeting had been chosen.

The date of this record makes it comprehensible why this topic was so charged with feeling. The session also showed that there were issues beyond the horizon of their personal lives about which they were anything but apathetic. That the introduction of this topic at this meeting was due to one man's misunderstanding was in a sense an accidental circumstance, but in another it was not, for the topic selected had been clearly announced by the leader and ignoring that fact was symptomatic of the group's inexperience in discussion procedure. It is also clear that the volunteer, as quasi-guest, was unprepared to cope with the situation in which she unexpectedly found herself.

But as a first experiment it was a useful experience in gauging the stage of the group in relation to planned discussions. There was much talk in the center about the conduct of the members in this first meeting, and much criticism of those who "couldn't discuss anything without getting so excited that they lost their tempers."

Therefore, a meeting was planned for the purpose of undoing some of the ill effects of this experience. After that the staff intended to drop the idea until more members were mentally and emotionally ready to participate.

For that second meeting a staff leader had selected as subject "The Rising Cost of Living." She reminded the group that they had not chosen a topic the last time. She then said they ought to have a few things about discussion groups clear in everyone's mind before starting. Everyone ought to have a chance to give their opinions. The chairman was there to see that everyone had this opportunity. This meant that everyone must ask the chairman for the floor and once granted, as a matter of courtesy, he should not be interrupted. There was much nodding in agreement at these rules.

The original attendance of sixteen had shrunk to nine. Among the seven who no longer came were Mr. Sullivan and Mr. Rothchild, as well as less vocal individuals whose curiosity in this new activity had been quenched by the previous session.

This meeting succeeded in substituting a more controlled procedure for the former free-for-all. The leader took an active role in giving reasons for limiting the scope of the discussion to one item of rising costs: namely, food; in gathering up the various comments and suggestions; in drawing everyone into taking a part; and at the end, in complimenting them on their self-control in waiting their turn before speaking. It was more than a practice session in procedure, for the first planning for a cafeteria at the center was made at that time, together with considerable informative discussion about cooperative buying and cooperative restaurants.

But three years were to go by before the accumulated experience of functioning together and the changing level of membership interests made the staff feel that a discussion group would now be an appropriate activity.

By then the center had been in existence six years. The membership was composed of a substantial core of charter members, whose individual self-confidence and corporate assurance had steadily grown, a factor which was having a stimulating effect on newcomers. Part of the corporate assurance came from the widespread interest in the center, the stream of visitors and the many speakers who confirmed the staff's claim that the club was demonstrating the abilities of older people. This was a very different climate in which to explore their interest in wider horizons. There were also, among the newcomers, many to whom discussion was not a new experience, for they had until quite recently been members of unions and taken part in their forums.

Though there was now little fearfulness of the outside community and much confidence in this environment, yet each new undertaking always involves first creating a group feeling among the participants, as well as clarifying, by eliciting from each new gathering, what they understand and are prepared to undertake as the purposes of a new activity.

To avoid any unfortunate associations with the early discussion group, this new feature was called "Current Events" and has now been in existence three years, with one change of leadership in that period. Attendance at the first session was thirteen, of whom only one was a woman and only one, Mr. Schulman, had been in the early group. Others of that first group were to join later. The then president, Mr. Manheim, came to the meeting, as did Mr. Edwards.

The worker explained that they had gathered to see if there were any subjects which would interest all of them, which they would want to discuss together, learn more about, and then, as a result of their joint talks and reading of newspapers, see if there were matters in which they might want to take action. She asked what subjects they would select.

The course of this first session is so indicative of the changes which had occurred in the past years that we would outline briefly what happened. One man suggested discussing health legislation since he and his wife were both ill and could not manage the added expenses on their welfare budgets. Mrs. Leaman demanded the floor and said something should be done about housing since she lived in such a terrible place. These personal histories were cut short by the next speaker, Mr. Haroff, who said that no one was interested in individual troubles as everyone had them, but they must discuss general topics and especially those about which, as a group, they could find remedies. The group quickly accepted this viewpoint and began discussing the Old Age Assistance program, and quelled as out of order Mrs. Leaman's further attempts to discuss her housing difficulties. Since the Governor had commented that day on Old Age Insurance, the worker now presented the newspaper clipping. Mr. Schulman read it aloud and the worker suggested they might get a speaker to inform them about the insurance plan and its suggested improvements. Mr. Haroff said he was well informed and offered to give a talk on the subject to which the members enthusiastically agreed.

Furthermore, they spontaneously undertook to make Mr. Edwards chairman of these meetings, put Mr. Haroff in charge of the next program, voted that the worker should be secretary and keep a file of any clippings and future correspondence and decided when and where the meetings were to be held. They were emphatic that it was to be held in the lounge, so that all the members would be exposed to it. Mr.

Haroff also said that in the future they must make contact with all other centers in the city in order to set up a city-wide organization to map out a program for the welfare of older people—and in time choose delegates to send to Washington for interviews with their senators and representatives. Mr. Edwards said they must also discuss transportation and how to secure improvement in the bus service, but was reminded that they had already settled on a subject for the next meeting.

We may take for granted at this stage the know-how of organizing the group; appointing officers, and settling the time and place of the meeting and the selection of a topic which were accomplished at this session. These procedures were the fruits both of experience in the club and of the competence of the newcomers, together with some steering on the part of the worker.

What was to develop into two trends, foreshadowing the future of these discussions, were both apparent in this session. One, as later months showed, was the inability of many members to translate their personal problems into terms of general issues. The other was the idea of becoming a pressure group.

In Mr. Haroff's case, who was the one to outline it here, this idea assumed the dimensions of a fantasy which he was soon to abandon, and with it all participation in the group, as soon as realistic obstacles could enable him to claim that the rest lacked the capacity to grasp and follow his leadership.

A third tendency, which was to recur periodically to the present day, was the desire to impose this activity on the total membership. It seemed that here at last they had found an interest which most promised to satisfy the need to still feel themselves effective adults. If some were either unwilling or too realistic to believe that they could become, as it were, a union of the aged, at least they could more directly satisfy their sense of having started an important activity by presenting it to an audience of their peers.

Though the worker records the comment that their enthusiasm far outran their understanding of the preparation necessary for what was to be a public demonstration of discussion, she bowed to their wishes, well aware that at this stage the impetus of their interest was more important than prosaic preparation.

She achieved that preparation by talks with individual participants and by arranging a small planning session of the group before they presented themselves in the lounge.

Mr. Haroff had suddenly taken offense during a private disagreement with one of the group and refused to speak. The worker, therefore, arranged to have an informed speaker preside at the discussion. This meeting set a standard of performance which offered an acceptable compromise between those who wanted all to be present at current events, and those who understood the values of a small discussion group. From here in, subject matter of assured general interest was presented to the general membership by invited speakers, as contributions to the program, sponsored by the current events group, and they were willing to confine particular topics to their small group meetings.

It was understandable that certain issues closely affecting their own lives would again change the atmosphere of these sessions. During the period of budget reductions, which spread consternation throughout the center, the sessions were crowded to capacity with individuals who never came before or since, but who were now eager for a chance to talk about this change.

At first, and for a long while, the pattern of these sessions became stereotyped. Each was a round of individual speeches about the price of milk, bread, eggs, closely listened to and loudly applauded. In the tide of feeling those who were not recipients were swept up and shared the agitation. Explanations of the interlocking responsibility of city, state and federal procedure in determining the level of budgets made no headway against their feelings.

It was at that time that Mr. Falk joined the group and continued his agitating speeches which intimated that a corrupt administration had engineered the changes and that he had access to political influences which would undo them. There were proposals from former union members to organize a march on City Hall.

This type of session went on for several months and slowly certain effects became apparent. First reactions which, in the lounge had been intensified by rumor, misinformation, and confusion, were here modified by facts and explanations. Feelings were relieved by being ventilated, especially for those who had never come to meetings before. The proposed march on City Hall was vetoed in favor of a less spectacular form of protest by letter to the Department.

But though the budgets were not changed, more was accomplished than merely relieving feelings. Once and for all, these sessions changed the shamed hiding of one's status as a recipient and substituted, during this distressed period, a sense of solidarity in openly discussing common problems. And sharing problems in turn helped one's personal readjustments.

The presence of those who were not recipients and for whom this topic presently became boring, together with the gradual acceptance of the new budgets, presently made it possible to introduce new subject matter, topics which ranged from local and national to international issues. Though the worker made many attempts to involve the group in determining the selection, asking them to bring clippings from their various language newspapers, few did so, and she was forced to take the initiative in the planning and preparation for many months.

But during this time the process of discussion as analysis

of issues, amassing of information, statement and justification of opinion, made considerable progress. A new competence in this direction became apparent.

The early tendency to personal orientation was also restricted. There are always individuals who continue to be personal and prolix, but the group is more experienced and soon points out that speeches must be brief and personal histories are out of order.

There have been recurring times when the group again felt that this was a superior activity which should be imposed on a greater number of members, as in the discussion of the card players. But here again a counterbalancing influence won. This faction pointed out that all their lives they had had to do what someone else wanted, they had had to obey a boss. Here at last in the later years they had a center where everyone was free to do as they pleased; people were different and here they should be allowed to follow their own bent. This tolerance and even appreciation of the values of difference, clearly formulated in this controversy, was another sign of moving ahead.

The early conception of becoming a pressure group also changed. The budget crisis played its part, but as that topic was left behind and many others less personal took its place, such as rent and price control, a more realistic understanding of their powers of social action as citizens emerged and such discussions generally led to letters to their representatives in the state, or national legislatures.

The most recent development was again a controversy between two factions in the group, those who rejected topics "which don't concern us," often placing in that category most local political, economic, or national as well as international issues, and those who protested they were interested in the widest range and valued their retirement as a time when they could pursue such interests.

Here again the worker used the device of appointing a

small committee, representing the opposing viewpoints, to work through these differences and at the same time capture the active participation they indicated.

There were four in this group and at the time the worker asked them to serve, these four had been the most articulate, and had ranged two on each side of the disagreement. That in the course of a few committee sessions their respective positions should again shift, one of them drop out and another member be added, was part of the astonishingly rapid results of this committee's talks.

The two who had argued for topics closely connected with the interests of old people were Mr. Fleitman and Mr. Seisal, and as was to be expected, for different reasons.

Mr. Fleitman, a former master electrician, who had recently retired, was a relative newcomer. He had had a wider experience than most of the members, which showed both in the breadth of his information, in his speech, and in his quiet, easy manner. His reasons for limiting the selection of topics were both realistic and practical. The current events group met only once a week, not long enough for what he felt to be the worker's educational goals. Nor could the members respond to such goals. But they could and would take part in a combination of discussion and information about matters which were within the range of their daily interests. He clearly understood the values of participation in this activity, and was, therefore, concerned to make topics correspond with the level of capacity.

Mr. Seisal was a less secure person than Mr. Fleitman, with a nervous, high-keyed energy. He had more need to use the current events group as an outlet and a means of self-assertion which found gratification in talking there. His criteria for selecting a topic were concerned neither with widening horizons, nor with stimulating group performance. Like his friend, Mr. Falk, the president, he felt that the center had great prestige and therefore so well-known an institution should find ways and means through its current events group of meeting the practical needs of the aged by securing special privileges. However, in the smaller group, after advocating special transportation passes, he was cagey in following up with other examples.

Mr. Gentz was also new and had come to the center after an illness. He had enough income to retire, but both his family and his doctor had worried over what he would do with himself when he had no work "to occupy his mind." He had always wanted to paint and he was fortunate in finding the center just when an exceptionally good teacher could give him instruction and confidence to try. Shortly afterward there was an exhibition in which he had two paintings. This encouraging beginning led him to explore other activities and to try "current events," which also interested him. His quiet, thoughtful comments were against limitation of topics. (We would like to interpolate here that the place he quickly made for himself in these two groups soon led to his selection as member-at-large for the executive committee, so that in a very short time he has found several interests to fill his self-chosen leisure.)

The fourth member of this committee, Mr. Wacksman, had spent several years at the center without feeling satisfied with the shop work, or the occasional tailoring services he was able to do. He had been in the garment trade and active in the affairs of this union local. At the center he had tried, both in membership meetings and in current events, to state what he felt so strongly were the new opportunities which retirement could mean. His soft voice, pink complexion, and mild manner, give no hint of the acute perceptiveness and constant reflection which goes on within. Both his English and his educational training are inadequate to fully express his thoughts, so that he had often been brushed off and quashed when he tried to develop them. Therefore, this controversy over the scope of interests represented the very crux of his dissatisfaction and what he felt were the undeveloped opportunities at the center and his position on the issue was unequivocal.

There were several immediate benefits to selecting these four to be a committee. It ended this session on a positive note at a moment when the group saw no way out of this split in viewpoint, for it implied that a solution could be found. It also acknowledged the leadership roles of the disputants and thus predisposed them to work together. And the first session gave the worker an opportunity to draw each one out more fully about his expectations, his criticisms, and his suggestions for this activity. It was also an opportunity to give them an understanding of the secondary values of current events as a means of introducing new members to interests and contacts, a way of making a place for one's self and getting confidence in this new setting. They had not thought of this aspect before and both Herzfeld and Gentz were especially responsive to this idea and were later to take it into account when discussing performance and how to improve quality.

The first committee session, besides elaborating their viewpoints, also concentrated on rules of procedure which would prevent the group from "splitting" into factions on a topic. This was Mr. Wacksman's special contribution, with some frank and friendly criticisms of the worker's "softness" in letting members ramble. The greatest achievement was that the committee volunteered to make themselves responsible for the selection of topics, to bring their suggestions to the committee meetings, and to discuss and brief themselves on the final choice.

It was settled that there should be a rotation of chairmen but they now foresaw that some would be less qualified than others and meetings would vary in performance for that reason. There was much agreement among the four over the question of methods and since it took up the rest of the hour, they were willing to meet once more before the next session for an agenda discussion. Since neither Mr. Herzfeld nor Mr. Gentz was eager to be chairman, and Mr. Seisal also held back, Mr. Wacksman promised to take over.

In the Agenda session Mr. Seisal was restive during the more probing discussion of suitable material. In the next one he was absent and then found excuses to drop out of this committee. He continued to speak in current events but there was able to select the situations in which he felt secure.

The next current events meeting showed a marked change of atmosphere. Mr. Wacksman opened with an excellent summary of the reasons for the new rules of procedure and why he proposed to be a "tough" chairman. The topic chosen was "Should the Proceedings of Congress Be Televised." During the lively arguments and considerations of its values, of the financing of such a service, and its benefits in greater citizenship participation, the chairman kept order, limited speakers, and held them to the point. The group was visibly pleased with his clear-headed and firm performance. When an habitual and rambling speaker was interrupted and was startled and hurt at being told to come to the point, the worker explained that the new committee had made this ruling against which she herself had often transgressed in the past, and to her astonishment he was able to condense his speech to a few brief remarks and was cordially applauded for doing so. There was not only lively participation, but many expressed their approval of this meeting. Mr. Wacksman was elated.

The following meetings were again well attended and there was much interest, though the next two chairmen were less able and tended to make speeches themselves rather than to function to guide procedure. Yet the fact that the topics were being selected by a membership committee suddenly seemed to stimulate the rest of the group to initiative in a way that the worker's many attempts had never succeeded in doing.

Presently Mr. Wacksman made two other suggestions. The first was that topics should be announced in the lounge two days before the current events meetings—so that people had time to think about it. They should then be again reminded on the day, just before the meeting.

The second suggestion was a meaningful modification of the rule of brevity. The object, he explained, was not that each person, or even many, have a word to say, but that a contribution of opinion or information be relevant and fully presented. Quantity should yield to quality, and if others still had much to say, that was an indication that the topic should be continued in the following meeting.

Through the next sessions both suggestions were put into operation. The agenda committee had selected the steel strike and government seizure, and the topic, twice announced, drew a sizable attendance. The argument over presidential powers and unions led to a spontaneous demand from the group that the subject be continued. In the following meeting the place of unions cropped up more frequently, so that Mr. Wacksman, who was again chairing, asked whether they should discuss unions, were they democratic or autocratic in method. There was immediate agreement.

As the worker was summarizing the points, the chairman added a smiling comment—that while the group liked their "moderator," and knew that she had a "fine education," about unions "she knew nothing." She agreed whole-heartedly and repeated the comment at the beginning of the next session, saying that in this meeting she would have to depend wholly on the group's knowledge and experience for the material of discussion. Here for the first time her function shifted. They could draw on their own information and did so to sketch in the broad outlines of the history of unions, their benefits, and also their adverse effects in some situations. Yet where such experiences were sharply contrasted she could point out the wider viewpoints of the problem, refer to the depression and the beginning of Federal measures of dealing with unemployment problems. This supplied a perspective which many had not reached, and speakers who had been angrily disputing each other's comments and arguments now saw a new synthesis of their disagreement. As a result they promptly made the deduction that the next topic should be social security as an issue which grew out of the national scope of the problem of one's earning powers and savings for old age. This was the third time in a row that topics for the next meeting had been selected from the floor.

Mr. Wacksman and many others were well aware of the new level of thinking and discussion which this marked. After several years of passive attendance and the constant effort of successive workers to spark the group into more active participation, it had suddenly appeared. We tried to account for the various factors which were involved in the change.

Our experience with all special interest groups showed the same initial lag. Nor were we willing to assume that this was specific to older people. Any collection of individuals who gather together for an activity will be doing two things at the same time: namely, relating to each other and trying out the activity. The two processes will be affecting each other, so that first the one and then the other will be gaining ascendancy. During the budget crisis when current events was jammed with members to whom discussion had the limited and specific objective of protest, and unconsciously, of letting off steam, the results were a strong group feeling through having talked together. When that topic was exhausted many dropped out. Those who remained were the ones who now also felt themselves a group, who had a less limited conception of what they wanted from the activity itself, yet very differing viewpoints of what should be discussed and also very differing abilities and backgrounds.

It was at this point that the worker, forced to take the initiative in selection, was groping for the level of the group's interest, and certainly made mistakes while trying. What Mr.

Herzfeld correctly sensed as her educational trend was an example. The fact that many of these older people passively accepted her choices for so long seemed to have been a waiting period during which their own critique was maturing. All along there had been those who sensed the difference between one session and the next, one in which participation came alive and one in which they were politely attentive to the worker's efforts. But it took the controversy to bring this critique into the open, so that she could at last scoop up this emerging leadership and have it take hold. The change in atmosphere as they began to put their own resources to work was unmistakable. It was more than a happy accident that just at this turn of the tide toward group assurance there should have been the comment on the worker's ignorance of unions, a comment which she took care to repeat because at this moment it served so well to underline their own resources. Procedural restrictions were understood, accepted, and then developed, even though they were stricter than those the worker had enforced.

The similarity of this change with that which took place in self-government when control shifted from staff to the group is unmistakable. There too, group control was accepted as evidence of adequacy and touched off response. In the same manner, as initiative in current events grew, the worker's area of functioning shifted, to draw together the contributions of each speaker, to soften the impact of disagreements, to set the tone of discussion, to point up and summarize, as well as always to protect and support the less effective member.

We note many similarities in the process of group learning in current events, self-government, and dramatics, the three areas in which progress was most notable. There was the same slow start in all three, the same dependence on the worker's activity, and as self-reliance developed, the same emergence of leadership in the group. But the goals of a discussion group are less specific and more complex than, for instance, dramatics. This may account in part for the long time which elapsed before lively participation set in. Another factor is the kind of members which current events attracts. The attendance fluctuates greatly for several reasons. The meetings perforce overlap with those of the dramatics group, which draws off some of the active participants as well as some of those members who have been at the center for years and go to almost all groups. But the core of present leader participants is made up of men who are newcomers to the center and recently retired and to whom this activity is a welcome continuation of the preoccupations of their active days. Moreover, those who are readers have profited by the changing attitude of the community toward older people. They do not think of their older years as living on sufferance as did our early members. Newspapers, magazines, the radio, everywhere are emphasizing their newly discovered capacities and the center itself is evidence to them of continuing opportunities.

Finally, the capacity to discuss is made up of many elements, background of knowledge and experience, confidence in speaking, ability to conceptualize, and the individual attitudes which determine whether speaking is predominantly for the purpose of illuminating a topic or the personal need to talk. That the group's new standards were being used to good effect was illustrated by the case of the rambling speaker who always wanted to address the meeting but who had been checked in a manner both kindly and uncompromising. Therefore the worker's efforts could now be shifted to the discussion itself, for difficulty in speaking, whether due to lack of confidence or inadequate command of the language, can be readily helped, both on the spot and behind the scenes. The larger import of a contribution could be pointed up and concepts introduced which linked each speaker's comments. In short, discussion as an activity had matured, both in method and in content.

CHAPTER THIRTEEN

Terminal Years

Through group records and examples of individuals we have been building up the picture of this growing community of the aged, its increasing numbers, its intricate structuring in regard to status, standards, and community control. These are the evidences of the social process by which all human beings function together. They fall into relationships of leadership and followers, of cooperation in some areas, of competition and struggle for preeminence in others, and of cliques which find their own niches within a hierarchy of status in an emerging social organization.

In the constant flux of factors which keeps this structure forever in a state of change, our picture of the whole, as an institution, has been one of development and growth. But now the reader who has followed us this far may begin to be doubtful. He will suspect us of a professional bias which has blinded us to the simplest fact of reality—namely, that senescence is a decline of functioning. He will object that we report as though skillful efforts to provide a maximally favorable environment could indefinitely hold at bay the signs of such decline. He will wonder if we fail to recognize the symptoms of senility, are omitting mention of the psychotic illness so frequent at this age; or, and most obvious of all, are leaving out the physical enfeeblement which finally makes attendance at such a center impossible .

Unless we answer these questions his growing skepticism will be justified. The institution, as a complex of interaction, does progress as each year goes by—and the same year leaves its marks on individuals. Hardening of the arteries takes its toll of the mind's adequacy; stiffened joints and damaged hearts, vision and hearing register the body's decline; and sometimes the inexorable summation of a lifetime of maladjustments does end in psychosis. These things we also observe. In some cases we have had eight years to watch their development. To some individuals they were years which carried them past the peak of a full and varied activity to that slow relinquishing of effort which ends in death. The reader has had glimpses of many individuals as they were momentarily highlighted by the shifting focus of our attention to various aspects of this community. Perhaps if we now give a consecutive account of some of these people through the nine years it will answer in part the question of what happens finally to those who come as members.

Mr. Lowden was already an outstanding figure in the club when the first professional worker met him. The reader will recall that he became the center's first president, that he attached great importance to this office, and how reluctantly he learned to share responsibilities, first with the other officers and later, when it was created, with an executive committee. His difficulties were in no wise due to failing mental powers. He had an excellent memory and, as attendance recorder, could recall the full names and often the addresses of most of the members in the first two years.

It was his tense, rigid personality, his need to seize this last chance to compensate himself for a lifetime of domination by his mother and then his wife, and for the disparity between his ambitions and his achievements, which made him so self-assertive, so aggressive toward the opinions of others, so intolerant of anything which seemed to infringe on his authority. When his term of office was over and a constitution had fixed the limits of its duration he might have found the change unbearable had not the worker implanted the idea in the membership that his experience now made his services valuable in other offices. At this time there were not many members who had leadership ability and the group readily elected him as vice-president. Following that the worker suggested a new office, that of Registrar and official attendance keeper, to which he was then elected. During his presidency he had already taken over the task of keeping these daily records, feeling that his superior handwriting made this a natural responsibility.

He spent each day at this task, printing the names in large type and took the sheets home to total. Some years later the U. S. Public Health Service made a series of tests on vocabulary and visual acuity, using a selected group of members as subjects and Mr. Lowden was included. One of the testers reported with amusement that these old people told tall stories, that a man with 20/200 vision in each eye claimed he took the attendance, a manifest absurdity since he was practically blind. He was astounded to learn that Mr. Lowden's claim was true and that his drive to be indispensable made him able to use this minimal vision.

In his second year as president he married one of the members, a stout, kindly woman who confided to us that she would have proposed to him had he not done so because he was "so handsome and refined." It was a fortunate choice as her admiration of him was equalled by her unremitting attention to his comfort. She found ways to soothe his touchiness and to mediate between him and those at whose actions he so often took offense. During one of his absences due to illness the staff finally captured the attendance sheets and had the names typed into a loose-leaf note book with date spaces for check marks. He was furious at this new system and threatened to take the matter up with the Board of Directors. But here too his wife explained the change to him as an evidence of the staff's unwillingness to overtax his strength.

It therefore seemed tragic that Mrs. Lowden did not outlive her husband but died suddenly of a stroke. Since then he has lived alone. The staff has made efforts to get him into a home, as he is now totally blind and his coordination is dangerously unsteady. However, he refuses to consider the idea. But a couple from the center visits him frequently and brings him to the birthday parties once a month where he is received with gratifying warmth. Recently another man from the center moved into his apartment as lodger.

It therefore seems fair to claim that this unadaptable old man has been sustained in the past eight years by the satisfactions and relationships which he gained from the center. He showed a tendency to confabulation in his later years, asserting, for instance, that he was the grandson of President Adams, a claim which his simple wife accepted with pride. It is impossible to say whether under less fortunate circumstances this tendency might have been an early manifestation of an eventual psychotic illness. All we know is that it is confined to such fantastic self-inflation and that despite his increasing physical infirmities, he is sane and well-oriented.

Patrick Malone was one of the cases for whom this community became the focus of his last years. He learned of its existence through a newspaper clipping and came some four years before his death when he was seventy-two. He was born in Ireland, had had a good basic education and was a skilled tailor who had his own shop for many years. He migrated to America in 1907 when his anti-British political activities began to get him into trouble.

He married and at the time we first knew him, was a widower with an only child, a married daughter. He had a sister in the city and a brother living upstate with whom he had lived for a time until the brother's illness and his own arthritic condition made him decide to return to this city. Ten years earlier he was left an inheritance in Ireland and returned there but found that he was no longer happy in his native country. He sold the property and came back to America. Later when his son-in-law had piled up heavy debts he paid them and then moved into his daughter's home. This left him with only $13 per month from his Social Security.

At the center he joined the poetry group where his knowledge of Irish poems and his own verses, together with his humor and genial personality made him popular. He also began painting, mostly religious subjects. When the dramatic group was organized about this time he was cast for a major part in the play and throughout the ups and downs of that group's advance toward a successful public performance, maintained his own steady poise and growing competence in his role.

It was only after he felt securely established at the center, however, that he was able to discuss his personal problems with a worker. He was unhappy over the tension in his home and his own inability to pay for his board. The worker suggested that he apply for Old Age Assistance but his daughter was opposed since she was unwilling to submit to the necessary investigations. She came, however, to discuss these problems with the worker.

She spoke of what the center meant to her father, the benefit to them all of having him busy throughout the day, that he was happier and complained less in the evenings and that his grandchildren admired his paintings and craft work. When the matter of public assistance was interpreted to her she agreed that the tension would be decreased if he could contribute to the food budget and finally consented to his making application. He was given an adequate grant and the expected good effects on his own morale and in the home resulted.

He was presently elected secretary of the membership and later joined the executive board. He also worked in the craft shop and his daughter saw his exhibits at the city-wide Hobby Show as well as his stellar role in the performance of the play.

Throughout his years as one of the editorial board of the center publication he wrote on many subjects and frequently contributed poems. The day that the news of Israel's statehood reached the center there was an impromptu celebration and Patrick Malone made a speech, one which further endeared him to this group from many lands. It went in part: "The Irish and the Jews have much in common—for they have a common foe . . . The Irish have been fighting them for seven hundred years . . . the Jews for only twelve . . . but in that time they've driven them out of Palestine, lock, stock and barrel . . . and I say that this victory is an honor on the altars of Israel."

His arthritic condition gradually became worse so that his legs dragged and his friends had to help him up the stairs. His speech became slurred. Presently he was bedridden, then came a stroke and he lay for some days in a coma. A day before the end, he suddenly rallied and wrote down some verses which he asked his daughter to send us. They were a tribute to the center, to its friendly atmosphere and to its activities. The last stanza read:

"I once was numbered, though not encumbered,
And favored as any there—
But now, alas, all seems to pass
When I can't go anywhere."

Many members in time are no longer able to look after themselves in furnished rooms and decide to enter a home for the aged. Sometimes they make this decision early and independently while they are still capable. But it is always a decision frightening in its finality and when the time of admission draws near they need support and the reassurance of talking out their feelings and again weighing the advantages of such a move. Others gradually can be prepared to accept the idea and be assisted in making their application. Some can continue in lodgings if housekeeping service is arranged for them.

A new home for the aged was recently opened in the borough and three of the center's active members applied for admission. The staff arranged to make the transition as easy as possible by conferences with the home's social workers. For several months these members returned for the birthday parties. Their glowing accounts of the fine rooms, excellent food and medical attention (". . . a three million dollar hotel with doctors and nurses to look after you . . .") did much to dissipate the dread of these institutions and indeed started a wave of applications.

These applications required much special counseling. Many had been hasty, prompted by an unconsidered impulse to get into such a desirable institution, whether or not an institution was indicated.

A case in point was Mr. Blatte, whose friend had been one of the three who had gone to this home, and who now wanted us to help him with an application. Though Mr. Blatte has a heart condition and poor eyesight he is still vigorous. He is a bachelor who has never made friends easily, nor even been able to get along with his siblings.

Therefore we asked him whether he thought he could get used to having a roommate at the Home. He was reminded of the fact that he ate in restaurants, choosing what he wanted and the hours he preferred to eat. This was contrasted with the fixed schedules of a Home. As he considered these adaptations he decided he greatly preferred his independence and dropped the matter.

The discussions about these applications were typical of those about old age homes which are frequent at a center. The older person, faced with some new problem which necessitates a change in his way of living, thinks helplessly that the only solution is such an institution. It is then a matter of determining which community resources or group of resources best fit his needs. He may still be able to live in his furnished room but needs housekeeping service. On the other hand he may be relieved to hear of the home care program by which he can continue to be independent but have the supervision and protection which this service affords. Or sometimes his problem is only with a specific room or landlady. By helping him to find another landlady and to have a place at the center his problem is solved. Older people often come to the center not because they want to become members but to ask about old age homes. They are surprised to find that from among this variety of resources more appropriate arrangements can be made for them. Not only is this important for the individual, but with the limited capacity of Homes it saves space for those who need this terminal care.

We have seen relatively few cases of pronounced senile deterioration at the center. We can speak only of those people who have continued to come over the years, and as in the case of psychotic break-down, there is no way of knowing the incidence of either of these possible terminal states among those who came for a while but whose prolonged absence we could not follow up.

The relative rarity of marked senility in the sense of glaring memory defects or inadequate behavior is notable. It is as though the social environment stimulated and sustained a social adaptation even if a closer scrutiny of the mental faculties might reveal damage. As long as the social behavior is acceptable there is a place for the individual. Yet contrariwise if social behavior breaks down the group is acutely rejecting.

Mr. Rosenberg came to the center six years ago at the age of seventy-three. He was then still able to secure an occasional day's work as a carpenter. Though he had no outside contacts and made no friends, at the center he played cards and was accepted by the others. But in two years he deteriorated rapidly. He became incontinent, was always irascible and subject to sudden outbursts of violent language. He preempted one small table as his own where, when he had no partners, he played solitaire. But presently, as no one would play with him, he was driven to roaming about the room, exploding almost daily at those who cold-shouldered him. The worker consulted with his Department of Welfare investigator to report his condition but his symptoms were not considered ominous enough to justify hospitalization at that time.

The situation was extremely difficult as the members insisted that he be debarred from the center, and the worker was forced to give him much individual attention. He listened to her explanations, "There are many people here . . . they can't all like each other . . . why should you upset yourself talking to those who don't like you?" But he answered angrily, "Should I walk around like a dead man and talk to nobody?" Anger provoked this bitter revelation of what it means to be cast out from the human circle.

This problem, so acute for a while, suddenly subsided when an increase in membership provided him with a new supply of partners. As a result he peaceably followed his daily ritual of games for some months. The final solution was sudden and tragic. He broke into his landlady's room one night, unclothed and in a state of confusion. She summoned the police and as he became agitated, they put him under restraint and removed him to a mental hospital where he died within the month.

In the past nine years the number of members admitted to a mental hospital has been conspicuously few. We have no facilities for accurate statistical studies. Our figures are drawn from the more than one thousand people who have been known to us over these years and of whose terminal history we were informed. Of these, three were committed following an organic illness. We know the details of only two of these cases. One, a man, was put in an institution following a cerebral accident. The other was a woman whose diabetes made it necessary to amputate her leg and who had to be committed following this operation.

There have been disturbed individuals who come to the center and whose mental condition betrayed itself in the first interview. But the two or three who have come left again as casually as they strayed in and we could learn nothing more of what happened to them.

There has been only one case of manifest psychosis among the many people who attend regularly. This was a woman who came daily for a period of many months, always sitting in the same place, quietly staring about her and ignored by the rest of the membership. She was unwashed and unkempt and sometimes had put on her dress backwards. One day she exploded in a delusional episode which caused considerable upset. She claimed that a wrist watch she saw another woman wearing was hers and had been stolen from her arm during the night when she was sleeping. The victim of her accusations was both frightened by her and at first unable to see the fantastic nature of these accusations. She was somewhat reassured the next day when Mrs. R. seemed to have forgotten the whole incident and again resumed her quiet staring. However, before the worker could arrange with the Department of Welfare investigator to have Mrs. R. examined by a psychiatrist she was struck and killed by an automobile.

But when we review these categories of terminal histories, slow enfeeblement, admission to old age homes, a few pronounced senile deteriorations and the rare psychotic breakdowns, we realize that the preponderance of our clients in the past nine years have died of a sudden illness. They have neither deteriorated mentally, nor have they become too infirm to attend. Their lives end before these symptoms of decline appear. In so large a membership these deaths occur constantly and at first the staff dreaded their effects on this community. But here too we had something to learn about old people. They were more realistic and less reactive than we. Death does not come as a shock to them—they have gone through this experience too often in their long lives. Nor do they dwell on its implications for themselves. It is as though they put it aside with a mild satisfaction in their own survival and continued to live in the expectation that there will be tomorrows like today. It was the staff, accustomed to working with younger clients, who had to adjust to the fact that at this age it is death which most often closes a case.

CHAPTER FOURTEEN

Counselling

Though the center is primarily a group-work agency, the
personalized help which is always a part of the group worker's function in facilitating group formation and the achievement of group goals, in a center for older people becomes
expanded into extensive counselling on individual problems.
There are several reasons why this is so.

Counselling is necessary because old people are confronted
with many and unfamiliar problems and feel their inadequacy to deal with them. They have more financial problems,
more health needs. They need glasses, dentures, diets, special
shoes, hearing aids. They have problems with their children,
difficulties in filling out forms to apply for public assistance,
or social security, or admission to homes. They are often
unaware of the many public services at their disposal, or do
not know how to apply for them. These are the common worries of old age. Yet old people have less contacts to which to
turn with their difficulties. Their isolation handicaps them
just when their problems multiply.

Thus, to become part of the center community not only
channelizes toward this new resource their need for activity
and social contacts, but their concrete problems as well. This
accounts for the diversity of situations which are brought to
the staff for counsel. Although our first responsibility is to
the group, the agency recognizes the special need for counselling service and allows time for it. Such service, however,

is not case work, even though the techniques and orientation
of case work are used.

There have been many examples of such personal conferences throughout this report. If we now add two more from
the many which might be selected, it is because each represents a typical stage of the later years, and illustrates the
interaction of this community's influence and that of a personal relationship to a staff worker in making a new adjustment.

The first refers to the stage of retirement, a problem which
is often brought to the center by older people who are not
members. They come because they have read of the center,
and not knowing where to turn for advice hope to find it here
after struggling alone with their worries and apprehension
about the future. Frequently they come to ask for help in
getting employment and while sometimes it is possible
through special agencies to place them, more often the real
problem is to help them to accept retirement.

Mrs. Dimrock had lost her job as a saleswoman, following
an illness. She was then sixty-seven, a trim, energetic woman
with two married daughters. In her younger years she had
been a piano teacher. When the depression came and many
piano teachers were available through the W.P.A., she found
it impossible to continue earning her living in this way. She
then worked in a department store. But now the long hours
on her feet were exhausting. There was no immediate financial problem as she had unemployment insurance and her
children could make adequate contribution. But her age and
her health (she had a thyroid condition) made it clear that
her working days were ending. Yet all her sense of personal
adequacy was invested in being able to earn. She spoke of her
friends who were well off, had husbands and comfortable
apartments, while she lived in a two-room walk-up. When she
was working she felt that she had a legitimate excuse for not
seeing them often, but dreaded a future in which this prop
to her self-esteem was gone.

She clearly needed help in making a readjustment. We

urged her to join the center, stressing how much she had to offer this community because of her musical ability. We explained its purposes and the changing attitudes toward a satisfying and creative use of leisure time. We introduced her to several women in the shop whose backgrounds matched hers. The results were astonishing. The women were friendly and congenial, and presently she invited them to her apartment. Her piano playing was an asset to the music group, and her first impromptu playing in the lounge was greeted with tremendous applause. She joined most of the special interest groups, poetry and dramatics, and was placed on several committees. Before Christmas her former employers called her back for three weeks of employment. When this was over and she had returned, she insisted on making a contribution to the center from her earnings. Since then she has accepted retirement and has adjusted to an income based on her social security allowance and assistance from her children without considering this a sign of failure. She has had a thyroid operation. She was able to face the serious illness and financial problems of one of her daughters with considerable poise, and to talk them over and accept the advice and help of the worker in easing them. She has achieved high status in this community and is absorbed in her many activities and relationships. Once, a year ago, she repeated to the worker a casual phrase used in that first discussion, saying "Do you remember when you told me perhaps I needed a new set of friends?" as though this comment had crystallized for her the whole concept of a re-orientation which she had made so successfully.

Our second case is an example of helping in the transition from active and satisfying participation in a day center to the more sheltered environment of an old age home. Here, too, the community as well as the relationship to an individual staff worker can supply important factors to mitigate the dread of this terminal step. In Mr. Schrader's case the center had given him an opportunity to cultivate his assets and to increase his self-confidence in a few years of living independent of his children. As his energy grew less, a home could therefore be presented to him as a means of eliminating unnecessary drains on his strength while enabling him to continue to do the things he enjoyed.

Mr. Schrader came to the center when he was 81, and immediately gravitated to the craft shop. He had always had considerable manual skill, but in recent years he had had no way of applying it. Therefore the space and the equipment of the craft shop were a welcome resource as were the variety of materials with which to work. He admired the metal work, but said he was too old to learn a new technique. When he was urged to try he learned quickly and was elated at winning a first prize in a city-wide hobby show for a copper fruit bowl.

Moreover, since he was a sociable person, who got on well with others, he enjoyed the new contacts in the shop and quickly made a place for himself in that group.

As his attachment to the club grew, he presently discussed his personal worries with one of the workers. He had three children—two sons and a daughter, and had lived for a time with one of his sons. He was not at ease in that household, "a daughter-in-law is different from a daughter" and because he felt himself an intruder he moved to a furnished room. His daughter married late and though he was relieved that she had done so, felt that her new relationship debarred him from living with her. His children contributed to his maintenance and he took care of his own needs by marketing, preparing his meals and cleaning his room. At first he merely mentioned these facts to emphasize that he was able to do these things as well as to demonstrate his competence in crafts.

Yet as he came increasingly often to chat in his mild and gentle way, or to present members of the staff with the colorful costume jewelry he carved and painted, these household chores cropped up more often in his talks as increasing burdens. Gradually the worker outlined the variety of possible living arrangements for the later years, home care, housekeeping service, and also old age homes, but sensed his abhorrence of the thought of a home. However, he came often to discuss these matters, especially as he began to find his daily chores increasingly taxing, and the effort to manage within his limited budget increasingly difficult.

She now gently explored his conception of homes and the reasons for his aversion. From a blanket dread of all institutions, he slowly began to balance specific features against his daily problems, fixed meal times and a set menu against the labor of choosing and preparing his own food. He said he was afraid of being cooped up with people he might not like. She pointed out that no group of people are ever all equally congenial, but reminded him of his popularity in the craft shop as evidence of his ability to get on with others. She described a modern home which had recently been opened and stressed that they were highly selective in their admissions, but that she was sure that his application would be accepted. She suggested that he visit the institution and pointed out that even though admitted to residence one could always leave if one were not content to be there. He inquired particularly about their occupational therapy department, intrigued by its diversified program and abundant equipment.

His children had long hoped he might consider a home but were afraid to mention it lest he take it as a rejection on their part. But it fortified Mr. Schrader's self-confidence to be the one to take the initiative about this plan and to present it to them.

He filled out an application and was soon accepted, as the worker had predicted. Yet it took six months before the advantages of the home began to weigh against his mounting difficulty in taking care of himself. It would free him of money worries, of the effort of travelling to the center, the quarters were new and beautiful, he could continue his handicrafts under the same roof, he could still visit the center, and two of his friends were planning to become residents just at this time. They too had children, yet did not consider this a deterrent to choosing this arrangement for their later years.

He has now made the change and for many months revisited the center frequently to tell his friends of his satisfaction with the home. He is active in craft work and continues to exhibit in the hobby shows.

Unlike most of our members whom we help to find ways of continuing to live in the community, or those others whose failing mental faculties make the protection of an institution

necessary, we recommended a home to Mr. B. solely to con-
serve his physical strength. His mental equipment was not
only not impaired but this frail and sensitive old man had
exceptional resources on which to draw. But they were being
submerged by his struggle to take care of himself.

Perhaps he has discovered the truth of the worker's claim
that his store of energy now can be reserved for the occupations he prefers. But his energy is also no longer being depleted by the emotional drain of conflict over making a decision and facing a change. This stress and strain could be
reduced by discussion and the support of his relationship to
the worker.

These were two major problems, but as a member turns
more and more to the center for his needs and satisfactions,
he inevitably brings his daily perplexities there likewise. This
concentration of interest makes for certain differences in
group work at a center for the aged. They are not differences
in principle but in effects, and we would stop a moment to
consider them. At other ages those who join groups do so as
only one of many activities. They go to school or to work,
have families and over and above these preoccupations, may
join unions, political organizations, educational classes, or
purely social or recreational clubs. These group affiliations
are, therefore, only a partial source of influence competing
with many other areas of interest. With older people membership in a community center is often the main source of
influence, almost the only dynamic factor in their depleted
lives. Moreover, for those to whom it has come to replace all
other social contacts its influence is not intermittent but
daily and continuous. They are driven to using it as the
major resource for creating a satisfactory existence.

Therefore, the effects of group activities and of interpersonal relationships are greatly intensified and constantly
carried over from one area to another. The reader will remember the examples of mass reactions affecting the whole

community. But there are more striking examples of intensified effects on individuals.

When Mrs. Applebaum first came to the center she was a meek, rather whining little woman, who spoke in a soft voice and was inclined to tears at the least provocation. She joined the dramatics group and was given a very small role. Yet her minor part in that successful production gave her such confidence that she lost her former timidity, and at the next birthday party, replied to her congratulations with a short speech, delivered in a firm, clear voice, and with conspicuous assurance. It would be hard to explain so great a change from this single instance of sharing in a group achievement except on the basis of the degree of self-fulfilling demands she had concentrated on this one activity.

The same concentration of demands can work negatively so that a disappointment suffered in this community can have effects which superficially seem out of proportion to their cause. Yet if all one's expectations have converged on one area these effects become understandable.

Sometimes the older person is prompted to bring his problems to the worker more in order to get attention than because he expects or urgently needs help with them. There are those who find it difficult to form relationships or to find a niche either in the center as a whole or in any special interest group. Yet in their need for ties they will use their worries as a means of attaching themselves to the worker, perhaps in response to her efforts to make them feel welcome and accepted in this new situation. She can then take advantage of these opportunities to involve them in a group, and as they are helped to link themselves with others through renewed satisfactions they will seek her out less frequently for individual counselling.

We remind the reader of Mrs. Mishkin whom the first worker found so rejected by the group and how she introduced her to a couple visiting from another club. It was inevitable that she should attach herself to the worker, bringing as her excuse many daily problems in order to feel reassured by the worker's attention. They were often matters which could readily be adjusted by methods which were unfamiliar to Mrs. Mishkin, or which she had been managing in some complicated way. So, for instance, she knew nothing of money orders and had been paying her fire insurance by making a long, exhausting trip to the company headquarters with the cash. Countless other worries were in the same category, but the worker used these personal contacts to also help her with her adjustments at the center. It was notable that as her "intellectual interests" found outlets in the poetry group and in her contributions to the center publication, these constant demands decreased sharply until today they are rare. Nor does she demand to be seen at once, as formerly, but will appear and volunteer to come at another time "when you're not so busy."

The change in Mrs. Mishkin's behavior should give us pause. Eight years ago her self-centeredness was her outstanding trait, yet in the intervening time it has not intensified but diminished. Last year she had a serious accident at the center in which she fell, breaking her wrist. A staff member took her to the hospital and when she was discharged, arranged for housekeeping service, and wrote or phoned her relatives and friends of her mishap. She weathered the shock and prolonged handicap of this accident with a poise which no one would have expected from her years ago.

On the surface such counselling service may seem to consist mainly of practical help, in giving information and making arrangements, of clarifying issues by discussion, of offering relief to feelings by making it possible to ventilate them in an atmosphere of understanding and patience and repeated conferences. But it is just in these many situations of counselling the aged that we have come to a better understanding of our role, an understanding which we cannot be content merely to indicate by the professional term "supportive." What the older person needs above all else is love and affection. He bears with incredible fortitude the severe adjustment to ill health, to failing faculties, to dependency with its many privations. The climate of the outside world through which he moves is indifferent or impatient or rejecting.

This community offers some escape from the weight of these many hardships, but more than anything else, as his hope and confidence revive, he craves the signs of affection. Nor are we the less professional when we understand and supply this need with greater freedom than we would allow ourselves with younger clients.

Throughout this report we have seen the repetition of one pattern of reaction—that the older person ventures toward new contacts, new activities, new experiences over the bridge of his dependence on a staff worker; that as he gains assurance in this community he then also brings his personal troubles to her for help; that in short, his security as a human being is revived by her acceptance of him, and that from this personal acceptance he can move on to further growth and new adaptations.

Just as the effects of group performance are intensified by the fact that the group's influence is daily and continuous, so our relationship to a member, being likewise daily, comes in a measure to replace the warmth of the closer ties he has lost. It is not relevant to determine whether we are cast in the role of a child, a parent, or a sibling. Such identifications are transient and their particular significance in the life history of any individual goes beyond the scope of our function with him.

But our scope does and must encompass this particular quality of warmth. Our colleagues from other fields of social work may question how one can demand of oneself a response of feeling of this nature. We can only reply that it comes into being as naturally as the need which appeals to it.

When we said in our introduction that the past nine years have been a shared experience of staff and members, we meant it in just this sense; that as we lived together day after day and saw and felt these growing relationships, our own deepened understanding spontaneously expressed itself as affection in all the many ways which are appropriate and natural.

This discovery of the dynamic importance to the aged of affection and acceptance again should not be news—any more than that they react on the same principles as all human beings. For years we have known that work with children depends on exactly the same thing. They accept our help and guidance in the stages of their growth only if it is conveyed in an atmosphere of affection. How much more must any work with the final stages of life require this essential ingredient of human relationship when those from whom one used to receive it are gone? One of our best adjusted members, a man of eighty-six, once told us, "The thing I find hardest in being old is to have outlived everyone whom I loved and who loved me." With children we can draw on our personal experience in helping them. With the aged we must depend on the sensitiveness of our observations which is heightened by that rapport which affection establishes. So for us too, it is an essential ingredient.

We come to this new field of social work dragging many of the influences of our culture within ourselves, and have often, in the past years, had to examine our own attitudes, when we suspected that they showed traces of its prevalent rejection of old people. Because these traces were masked it was all the more necessary to recognize them.

The reader has followed the changes in this community from an initial insecurity and extreme dependence on staff to an independence and the growth of community control. He will recall the stage when the members began to demand greater strictness of control over membership behavior, and the staff's hesitation in yielding to these demands. Just as there was an unconscious drive for dominance at work in the individual leaders who expressed these demands, our hesitation had reciprocal unconscious elements of overprotection. It was just in this tendency to overprotect that we recognized one trace of rejection, for overprotection is a denial of adequacy, of the right to self-determination, or even to make one's own mistakes.

It is obvious that this symptom of an unconscious rejection refutes the acceptance which we have been stressing as necessary in this work. It is for that reason that we record it here because this self-scrutiny marked another stage in our professional learning. We wish to make it clear that this latent contradiction in attitudes applied only to our clients as a whole group and was influencing our thinking and actions only in that mass situation. It was not a specific factor in a direct relationship with any one older person. One's attitude toward each single personality is determined by that individual as a human being and his age is only one of the many elements which enter into one's relationship to him. But finding this symptom of a hidden rejection made it possible to eliminate its influence. It also helped us to be more quickly aware of the meaning of certain difficulties which students in training often showed in their work.

Some of them were well-trained group workers, yet at first could not see that the group-work approach had any validity with older clients. For long periods they were unable to observe that the same processes were at work here as in any other age group. Their preconceived ideas about the aged blinded their observation and they overlooked motivations and reactions which in younger clients would have been meaningful and significant.

If we realized that we had unconscious blocks to seeing the meaning of new trends in group behavior, then it became understandable why more naive workers showed extensive blind spots in beginning work in this field.

Most of all it explains why inexperienced volunteers in all innocence think that "busy" work, passive entertainment, and "making them happy" are adequate goals for the many clubs for older people which are springing up throughout the country.

This evidence of lingering cultural prejudices in ourselves made us conscious of other examples of such influences, even though we ourselves were not guilty of them. We came to see that various common attitudes toward the aged stem from the same source. Overpraising performance whether in crafts or in any other achievement meant that they were being put in a special category, segregated from realistic standards. Doing things for them rather than enlisting their capacities as fully as possible, was another sample of negating whatever adequacy they had. And finally, using the short-cut of authoritativeness, instead of the slower procedure of arriving at decisions and plans by the process of group discussion and group participation.

We became aware of the significance of these attitudes because we encountered them so often during the past years as the community at large was discovering the aged. They appeared where there was no first-hand experience of the actual capacities, needs and special problems of older people. Thus these attitudes were not surprising, for preconceived ideas are only displaced by factual knowledge, and it was a preconceived idea that the aged have ceased to change and grow.

As we conclude this survey of our experience we are acutely aware that these records are the merest beginnings of factual knowledge. As practitioners we constantly had to act in situations without then, or often later, being able to isolate the many factors which were involved. We had to be content to note what we knew of the situation, to record our steps and to observe what followed. Our professional training in group and case work furnished a body of principles which not only had constantly to be translated into flexible practices and skills, but this practice was also an experimenting in adaptation to the unknown elements of this particular situation. Practice always requires flexibility but never more so than when techniques are being used both for the goals for which they were designed and at the same time for exploring the reactions, capacities and needs of the clients to whom they are being applied.

For instance, where it seemed that the level of comprehension of this group was widely uneven because of differences in schooling and/or language difficulties, we could not afford to forget that a recreation center for old people encompassed in its age span two generations. Our membership at one time included a father and son, and an uncle and nephew. What might interest and concern a seventy year old, would leave a client of ninety indifferent. Yet since the satisfactions of these members depended on their being able to function together as a group, we had to discover what common denominator there might be to bridge this span.

In this case, as with so many other factors of difference, it was the need to belong to some community which was more powerful than the difference of interest or capacity. The able ninety year old who came because of this need (and only the able could make the effort to come) was accepted and even made much of by his juniors because of his reassuring example.

As we review in our minds all that we have seen happen at this center, this need to belong seems the key to its evolution. To those who have family ties, as well as to those who have none, it is at present the only resource society offers where they can continue to function in a normal give and take with their fellow men. It is the exceptional few who, in their later years, can assert their capacity to do so amid the general public. For the rest, a center furnishes the social milieu which they have lost and which, no matter how rich the individual's resources, no one can recreate single-handed.

Yet the group life which such centers offer the older person does not and cannot duplicate normal community life. The social environment is both less diversified and more protected. This has some advantages. It screens out many of the demands which may be beyond the capacities of older people and thus shields them from a mounting sense of inadequacy. Yet it does so at the expense of other factors, namely the wide variations in individual need and capacity.

But so long as it remains the only simulacrum of community living, programming will challenge our resourcefulness and imagination to the utmost. For on such centers falls the burden of recreating for our clients some measure of the fullness of life. They have shown us that change and growth have no age limits. When the community at large makes this same discovery it will and must find ways to make use of the resources of the aged, and to find those tasks of participation and contribution of which they are still capable. For our clients have also taught us that human development occurs where it is nourished and sustained by contact with one's fellow men. Though we know that solitary confinement is the punishment most dreaded by criminals, the full significance of that fact came home to us when these older clients starkly demonstrated that self-confidence, skills, even sanity and attachment to life itself wither away because society likewise condemns them to isolation.

Such centers are only a beginning in restoring to the old the right to live life to the end with the fullest opportunity to use one's capacities. How sorely they have missed that right was made plain in the words of the old man who said, " 'Tis the blessing of God to find such a place, for do you know that you can die of loneliness."